For dear Simin Joon,

With gratitude,

Pari

Vancouver,
June 2016

MY BLUE CANVAS

Life and Art
Memories and Meditations

Text and Artworks: Pari Azarm Motamedi
Project Director: Massoume Price
Editor: Freydis Jane Welland
Graphic Design: Flora Navaee
Photography: Hamid Zargarzadeh, Robert Keziere,
Patrick Hattenberger, Roya Darvish, Mahgol Mortaheb

Library and Archives Canada Cataloguing in Publication
Azarm Motamedi, Pari, author
        My blue canvas: life and art, memories and meditations / Pari
Azarm Motamedi.
Poems and art works.
ISBN 978-0-9809714-7-7 (bound)
        1. Azarm Motamedi, Pari. I. Title.
ND249.A97A4 2016   759.11   C2016-901506-8

Published by Anahita Productions Ltd.
Vancouver, Canada

www.anahitaproductions.com
info@anahitaproductions.com

Printed in Canada by Friesens Canada

MY BLUE CANVAS

Life and Art
Memories and Meditations

Pari Azarm Motamedi

Anahita Productions Ltd.
Vancouver, Canada
2016

For our grandchildren

My wish for you is to thrive in and benefit
from the most beautiful aspects
of your multicultural family
Swiss-American and Iranian-Canadian.

And for all the children and grandchildren of immigration
residing all over the globe
may you be inspired
to know and cherish the positive attributes
of all your cultures
the ancestral and the adopted.

Table of Contents

Part One
Memories and Meditations

Part Two
Artworks

Gratitude

This book is a gesture of gratitude
for all I have been so fortunate to have in my life
my parents
my spouse and sons
my sister
my family and friends
teachers and mentors on three continents
poets and writers who inspired me
artists and craftsmen who opened my eyes to beauty.

This book is in your hands
because some very special people
gave me their complete support and trust
offered me their knowledge and above all their friendship.

Massoume Price
My dear friend and publisher
I am truly thankful to you for your
complete and valuable guidance in supervising this project
with utmost care and competence
at a time when you had more important issues on your mind.

Freydis Jane Welland
My sensitive and inspiring editor
I am deeply grateful for all I learned from you
for your encouragement and kind and thoughtful editing.
I greatly enjoy our reflective collaborative journeys.

Flora Navaee
My talented and capable friend and graphic designer
I am very thankful to you for offering your design expertise
and for working with me on this book
with as much patience and caring as if it were your own.

To all the excellent photographers
I offer my wholehearted thanks to each of you
Hamid Zargarzadeh, Robert Kezier, Patrick Hattenberger
Roya Darvish and Mahgol Mortaheb.

To my cherished friends and family who read parts of the book
and to Diane Gooderham who read it all so diligently
I am thankful for all your valuable comments.

Sheereen Price
My young and talented friend
thank you for proofreading the book with care and a fresh outlook.

I am grateful to all of you
my beloved family and friends all over the globe
who have been with me in this journey of life and art
and who have encouraged me to create this book.

Yasmin
My most profound gratitude is to you my granddaughter.
You are my inspiration for writing this…

Why this book

Away from Iran
living in a city on the shores of the Pacific Ocean
I also dwell
every single day of my life
somewhere else
somewhere in the borderless
placeless culture of a country and a people
I left behind decades ago.

Its poetry
music and visual arts
inspire and sustain me.
Memories of my childhood within its borders
continue to influence and affect me.
The everyday hardship of its people
their pain and desperation
deeply distress me.
The mostly negative depictions of it in the media
demoralize me.

My art
a personal bond
drawn
painted
pierced and hammered
into paintings and pieces in precious metals
keeps me connected with my culture.
It has been my therapy
my solace and sanctuary.

This book is a statement
of gratitude and appreciation for the culture
community and family that have sustained
nourished and inspired me and all my work
an expression of how this culture
has influenced my art
the content
the themes
the forms.

Windows

Windows fascinate me
those openings through which one can see
beyond the world of the present
near and immediately accessible existence.

Viewed through the multi-coloured
leaded glass windows
of the Persian courtyard houses
the world beyond changes
with the distance from the window
or the colour of the glass.

From afar
I look through
colourful windows of memory to see
once again
the signs
sights and sensations that inspire me
glimpses into experiences
that shape me and my creative work.

My childhood and youth in Iran
were not so different from others in my generation
living in middle class urban families.

But each ordinary existence
has elements that make it unique
experiences that shape it
chances and choices that alter its direction.

Mine was a protected childhood
centred on family and school
household chores
and exposure to art and culture.
Discussions of politics and religion
were not encouraged
were almost absent
although I grew up in a time
of significant political events in Iran.

Looking into the distant past of my childhood
I tell the story
up to more recent times
sometimes up to the moment of writing.
Memories and thoughts
do not completely obey
delineations of time and place.
The past mingles with the present
and hints of thoughts about future days
yet unknown
find their way into
the frame of the window.
The act of looking
through these windows of memory
writing about what I see and feel
explains why and how my creative work
of the past thirty years has evolved
from the sensibilities
experiences and insights
rooted in my Persian cultural heritage.

The aim is to illuminate elements of my cultural assimilation
grounded in a distant past
in the lives of generations of my ancestors.
I write about people and places in my life
about nature and gardens
even about objects.
These are stories not in any chronological order
but pieces of a puzzle making a whole.
I write in the form of lyric prose
perhaps in free verse or in a nameless form
with no punctuation marks except the full stop
and the occasional question mark.
It seems as if form emerges from feelings
at the moment of writing.

Between the windows there are pages for reflection
for the eye to rest
for the mind to experience a quiet moment
a chance to contemplate.

These images in words
seen through the transparent canvas
of windows of memory
allow me to narrate the moments of a life
moments of joy and pain
love and loss
leaving and arriving
emotive and life changing moments
inspiring and motivating my creative work.

The views from the windows
lead me to 'Contemplation in the garden'

a meditation on life and art
taking me to a place beyond words
the world of forms and colours
and my artworks of a lifetime.
The predominant language becomes
that of my art of the past thirty years
inspired in its entirety
by the artistic and cultural heritage of Iran.
My artworks in many media
paintings
games
jewellery
items of furniture
all belonging to the present
rooted in the past.

PART ONE

Memories and Meditations

Old roots and new roots

■ I am Iranian.
A statement of fact
repeated with conviction
and a certain sentiment of well-being
a very normal answer to a question.

Iran is my country
a phrase uttered without hesitation.
The rich ancient soil gave me roots
deep into distant time
wide into vast territory.
The colour of its blue sky
etched itself in my mind's eye
as the bluest blue.
Dry rugged mountains
bordering the desert
evergreen hills
on the rim of the Caspian Sea
were the backdrop
of my dreams and my days.

I come from the land of the poets.
The poetry of Khayyam and Rumi
Hafez and Sa'di
has been recited for centuries by my ancestors
recited by grandparents and parents
aunts and uncles gathered in a room or in a courtyard
on warm and sweet smelling summer evenings.
I learnt these poems in primary school
and knew them by heart
copied them in small lined notebooks
with a reed pen dipped in an inkwell.

I come from the land of Persepolis
Persian gardens and Persian rugs
from the land of pomegranate gardens
and orange persimmon trees.

But alas
this land that I love
also had prisons and patrols
and people who lost their patience
people who yearned and fought for freedom
and found themselves instead in prisons
no matter which powerful men ruled them
and under what names.

As the contradictions and contrasts
the desolation and dissatisfaction grew
disparate groups
who had never truly understood each other
who did not speak the same language
who did not dream the same dreams
came together
almost overnight.
Change was what they all wanted
and change was what they got
a change
no doubt
and not much more.

Some in this land that I love
still followed their dreams
and still faced dismay and distress
and often much more.

Others
strong and determined
withdrew from the newly emerging
poles of power and money
into the solitude
of vocations and occupations
that always matter
that always bring real change
slowly and gradually.

They persevered with patience
the hardships of war and everyday life
tirelessly
teaching
writing
making art
promoting cultural endeavours
supporting and healing those in need
carrying out everyday responsibilities
striving for a peaceful life
yearning for the elusive
seemingly more and more unreachable freedom.

Some others
who also yearned for freedom
for themselves and their children
fearful of fighting
fearful of war
and what the future could bring
one day
packed up and left
as did we.

We arrived in Vancouver
on a cold November night
decades ago
our family of four
my husband and best friend for life
our two young sons
ten years old and four years old
to start a new life in a new land.

What am I now?
Still an Iranian?
A Canadian?
An Iranian-Canadian?
Does it matter?
What about our children?
Do these things matter for them?
Will it matter for their children?

I have slowly and consciously grown new tender roots
new affinities and friendships
have experienced painful and joyful events
that bind and connect me
with this new land of evergreen mountains
on the rim of these tranquil blue waters.

I did not know when we left
that in this new home I would encounter
the most devastating experience of losing a son
and the darkest grief that
burnt and hollowed me to the core
opened my eyes to the unpredictable
ephemeral nature of life and changed me forever.

It has been nineteen years.
I have slowly climbed out
from the absolute darkness of grief
the shadow forever the background of my life.

The compassion
dedication and caring
of my family and friends
my newly made friends
my meditation group and yoga community
and the kind and caring people of this land
held me through the grief and the healing.

Joyful events and memories are numerous too
binding me to this new land
family gatherings and trips
school performances
camping and tennis tournaments
soccer fields and rugby fields where our sons played
sports days and graduation ceremonies.

Family celebrations and weddings
have brought much joy to our lives
and most of all
the marriage of our younger son to the beautiful
wonderful woman
he would not have met
had we not left.
I have cherished these blessings
and am grateful for experiencing
the unmatched happiness of being a grandparent
in our new home in this vast country.

I have found the contentment
of creating and exhibiting art
in this calm and peaceful city.
I have discovered the gratification of offering my art
for causes I believe in and care about.

New roots are cautiously growing in this soil
that has been our home
for the last thirty-two years.

But still I am drawn to that placeless place
with no geographic borders
a place I found in the lines of poetry
songs
images
colours
and memory.
A place discovered
in the freshness of childhood and youth
a place I have always found
a place I have never lost.

How free I feel
to be able to see
from this distance
what I have left behind.
How free I feel
to be able to choose and cherish
from this distance
what is enriching and beautiful
positive and humane
and leave the rest.

I come from the land of the poets
the land of great architects
and master craftsmen
the land of soulful musicians
the land of the wise and the kind-hearted
the land of delightful gardens
and magnificent mountains.

My heart still aches.
Still after all these years
some nights are sleepless with thoughts
of what could have been and what is.
I still care and cry for the land and the people left behind
but I know my limitations
and have now embraced my new identity in this new land.
In this world full of turmoil
I am aware of my fortune
of living with my small family in this tranquil city
immersed in two cultures
nourished and enriched by both.

I am Iranian and Canadian.
This is now my answer to the question.

Two Shores, Two Trees

Watercolour, acrylic ink
75 x 38 cm
2004
Artist's collection

Dissonance and harmony

■ He was born seven years before the start of the First World War
in a traditional family in Isfahan
in the world famous city
the pearl of Persia
with the boundless blue skies and brilliant blue domes
and a river brimming with water.

I can picture him in my mind
six years old
small in stature
pensive beyond his age
in grey pants and jacket two sizes larger
following in small light steps
his mother in full *hijab*
walking through the mud-brick
labyrinthine alleyways
in the crisp
early morning sunrise of an autumn day.
He is her only child.
He will be my father.
She will be my grandmother
my *Bibi joon*
taking him to his first day of school.

Before the end of the first lesson of the day
I see him again
seemingly smaller in stature
more pensive
a lump in his throat
tears in his eyes
following a scolding father
in small reluctant steps.

I see my grandfather
leading my father
away from the more modern school
through the mud-brick labyrinthine alleyways
to the traditional clerical school.

   My grandfather conventional
   austere religious a merchant
   in the Isfahan Bazaar opposing
   all that was new or unknown
   saw the life of his then only
   son our father within the old
   known ranks of the clergy or
   in the old labyrinths of that
   familiar bazaar he knew. He
   was incapable of seeing that
   there could be another future.

My grandmother
a divorcee
after only a few years of married life with him
was a rarity
a rarity in the Iran of a hundred years ago
in the Iran of the Qajar kings.
In our father's words
a modern woman for those days
she wore the traditional *hijab*
black from head to toe
prayed and respected the rules and rituals of her religion
but saw another future for her son
wanted to give him the chance of a different life.

The ritual of the first day of school
repeated for several days
the interruptions
the walks back and forth
from one school to the other
the scolding and the tears.
Finally both the schools
fed up with the disruptions
decided to put a stop to the untenable situation
asking the parents to make a choice.

The furious father
seeing the persistence of the mother
her resolve in determining the course of her son's future
and disagreeing with her intentions
attempted to take away the young child.
The religious court sided with him.

Not willing to give in she approached government authorities
sought help from influential relatives
argued through reasons unknown to me
and gained the custody of her only child.
She put him in the school of her choice.
Monthly support payments by the father
hardly covered the cost of the meals.
A single parent working as a seamstress
she played the role of two
with love and with discipline.
It was not easy to make decisions
to earn a living
to question and go against traditions
to follow her vision for the future of her son.

I have a feeling that the sad memories
of the first years of his life
stayed with our father
haunting him into adulthood and old age.

The chance that changed his life came at age fifteen.
Reza Shah
having put an end to the Qajar dynasty
and on a mission to modernize the country
needed educated individuals for this endeavour.
Our father was one of the students sent to France for university studies.

In Europe for nearly twenty years
fluent in French and English
with a degree in agriculture from France
and a doctorate in genetics from Edinburgh University
he returned to Iran.
Our grandmother had patiently endured
the hardship of the long night of the twenty-year separation
to make possible a better future for him
and for generations to come.

At Tehran University he began to teach genetics and biology
established a publishing company and bookstore
dedicated to medical sciences
devoting his life to learning and teaching.

In marrying our mother
he was lucky to find the partner
with whom he would create the harmonious family life
that as a young child he must have longed for
but had not experienced.

I was born in the first house they bought
a brick house with a courtyard.
Almost three years later
my sister and sole sibling was born in the same house.
Only in my later life have I realized
it was because of his own childhood experience
of dissonance and discord
that he was intent upon making the childhood experience
of his children
one of harmony and happiness.

He lived and worked in Iran
to the age of seventy-three.
Like many in his generation
he saw the prospect
of a promising future for his country
through better education and work
and did his share towards the realization of these aspirations.
To this day
ten years after his departure
his students
men and woman with greying hair
residing and working all over the globe
as accomplished physicians and veterinarians
speak of him with fondness and respect
remembering his sense of humour as well as his strict conduct.
Perhaps the deep and distant experiences
of the small pensive six-year old
in those first schools had equipped him
with an internal personal pedagogy
that was a mixture of humour and discipline
and which worked so well with his students.

Thirty-five years ago
at age seventy-three
saddened and disheartened by the events
taking place in Iran
concerned about the future
he initiated the immigration of the family.
West Vancouver became his home
for the last twenty-five years of his life.

At age ninety-eight
in full command of his intellect
and his emotions
with a body ravaged by old age
on a hospital bed
the final words he struggled very hard
to whisper to my husband and me
were the words of a poem by Sa'di.

    Neither riding on a camel
    nor burdened
    with a load
    like a mule.

    I am not the lord of a peasant
    nor the slave
    of the sovereign.

He died a happy
liberated man and was giving us
his last precious gift
telling us how he had reached
this state of peace and contentment in his life.

In her hands

■ She was born to the second wife
of a father she would never know.
She was his only child.
He lived for four months after she was born.
Her mother remarried within a few years
but she had a happy childhood
loved by her mother and stepfather
half siblings and the first wife of her father.

With a ninth grade education
and skill in the arts and crafts of her time
she got married at age sixteen
to a second cousin
just back from Europe
employed to teach at the university.

She was very young.
He was more than twice her age when they married
but they caught up with one another
she
learning everything and growing
he
young at heart
a willing partner and friend for her and her joyful
endless endeavours.

They loved each other
became good friends
had almost sixty-five years together
a happy life to the very end.

She lived for five more years after his passing.

Mother loved life.
She was full of joy
loved to create
to invent
to find a better way
to carry out any chore.
Nothing seemed too difficult.
She became completely
absorbed with the task at hand
a simple game
a school assignment
a sewing project
a new recipe
the repair of something that did not work.

She loved to teach
was a little impatient if we were slow to learn
expected the best from each one and all.
She kept us
my sister and me
on our toes from a very young age.
Somehow she made it all enjoyable.

In her hands
the simple piece of fabric
became the little dress
I wore as a young child
for an early family photograph
one of many dresses
that she made and I wore
over the years
into my adulthood.

In her hands
the yarn became
the identical small white sweaters
my sister and I wore
one year for Nowruz
the Iranian New Year
the sweaters with the dark red knitted motifs
around the neck and sleeves
worn with fluted
dark red knitted skirts.
More yarn was knitted
into many more pieces
for many cold winters.
Years later she created
blankets and cardigans
hats and scarves
for her grandchildren.
And still years later
on the shores of the Pacific Ocean
with fingers deformed with arthritis
she made knitted pieces
for my sister's grandchildren
her own great-grandchildren.

Decades ago
the small blankets
and the white cardigan
she knitted for our two sons in Tehran
were packed and came with us to Vancouver.
Our sons had outgrown them
but the pieces came here
kept in the silence of a suitcase.

These pieces will be mother's gifts of knitting
to our granddaughter
the great-granddaughter
she did not live to see
each piece imbued with her endless love
her generous spirit.

In her hands
every occasion would become a work of art
suffused with her endless passion and creativity
the celebrations of Nowruz
weddings of her grandchildren
gatherings of friends and family
cooking of meals
baking of traditional Persian pastries.

Shortly after settling in West Vancouver
she started to take lessons in the art classes
offered at the neighbourhood community centre.
So in her sixties
in a new home on a new continent
she took up painting and pottery
and furniture restoration.
She created vibrant watercolours
delicate clay vessels and fantastic clay fish.
She restored an old broken Chinese Chippendale chair
bought from a market
into a charming piece of furniture
that has sat in our living room
for the past thirty years
for me a symbol of her talent
her resolve to learn.

She exhibited her work
in the Cultch
the contemporary arts theatre and gallery in East Vancouver
and in group shows
in the West Vancouver community centre.
Her clay pieces now adorn every table and shelf
in our small house.
Perhaps our grandchildren
will one day get to know
their great-grandmother
through these creations in clay
and other samples of her work
which may survive into a distant future.
A future she will not know
but a future that she will continue to affect
through what she has left behind
both the tangible and the intangible.

For her the loss of our son
her grandson
was the unbearable shock.
Irregular heart palpitations
and numerous emergency room visits began
and thirteen years later a blood clot in her brain
caused the stroke that ended her life.
For thirteen years she had endured it.
She had submitted to this loss
with a certain grace
a certain surrender and acceptance
her strength of character
a model for many in her circle
of extended family and friends.

But the broken heart had never healed.
I found her many times
behind her sewing machine
sitting in the silence and seclusion
of her basement sewing room
with a needle and thread in her hands
a piece of fabric on her lap
and tears in her eyes.
Mother was her own art therapist
the sewing projects
the paintings
the clay pieces
her patience stones.

To the day of her passing
at age eighty-five
and despite everything
she seemed able to tap into a boundless
reserve of energy and creativity.
She still inspires me every day
to go beyond my doubts
and my limitations
to get in touch with a part of me
that can see and sense beyond all the pain
the beauty of life
and the intrinsic rewards
of creative work.

Love and life and music

■ Floating
the bow
touching
gliding over the vibrating strings
soaring sound
softening the space
the silence
for a second
for a moment
I am nowhere
somewhere
in a garden.

Something is said
sensitive
serene
not in words
but in sounds
in silken waves and waves of sound
from a mysterious place
sublime
seeping in
something elusive
sunny
sad
a conversation.

The memory comes back.
Abruptly
with the stilling of the bow
and the hand that guides it
the sound is no more.

Only silence remains
and a mysterious feeling.

I am mesmerized
with this music
this highest form of art
this abstract
mysterious and complete experience.
The music has just stopped
I am longing already
for this new
nameless
experience.
What happened?
How did it happen?
Where did it go?

An experience
of more than half a century ago
still present and vivid for me today.

I was fourteen years old
when I heard him play the violin
in a garden.
He was seventeen.
We played chess in that garden.
In the years to come
we listened to music
read poetry
and sat in silence together.
We talked
argued and discussed life.

He left to pursue his studies in Europe.
I stayed behind to finish mine.

We wrote each other letters
for many years
talked and contemplated and discussed life
on pages and pages of paper
each letter taking weeks
to travel the physical distance between us.
We discussed life and what we would build
naively
not knowing how little we knew of what life would bring
how it would be dictated
by chance
and not only by our choices
but also by choices that others would make.
We did not know how history
upheavals and revolution
would change our lives
and our dreams.
We did not know the fate that awaited us
the experience of the most terrible loss.
In those letters there was only hope
and dreams and noble intentions.

My violin player became my husband
the love of my life and my best friend
my companion
lifelong solace and support
everyday and always.
He became the father of my children
sharing with me the amazing

the immensely fulfilling
the baffling
confusing
challenging
experience of parenthood.

Before we left Iran
in the midst of the years of turmoil and change
he started to play a new instrument.
The *setar* became his intimate
soft-spoken companion
for hours and hours every day
his connection to beauty and truth enduring
despite everything
the music filling our home
showing me the healing power of art.

His quiet complete caring
his peaceful presence and support surrounds me
gives me the courage and the freedom
to pursue my creative work.
With the mind of a scientist
and the sensitivity of an artist
he is my mentor and critic
inspiring me to continue to work.

We have shared our life together
for almost fifty years
this unique life
this ordinary life
this life of love and much joy
and the greatest of all pain.

We have experienced together
the devastating grief of losing a son.
How did we survive this for these many years?
It seemed impossible in the beginning.
We have talked
lamented and cried
meditated and finally surrendered to this reality.

We have changed.
There is more awareness
to be present
'to love and be loved'
honouring the words
our son spoke a few months before he left us.

I am grateful for our blessings
and thankful for what we have
our younger son
who at age sixteen
with the loss of his brother
matured beyond his age
suddenly became a man
aware of the ephemeral nature of life
appreciative of its precious moments.
I am grateful for the man he has become
for the experience of seeing his loving family
and for becoming a grandmother.

More than half a century has passed
since the day
those first notes filled the moments
of that afternoon in the garden in Isfahan.

I am in the studio painting
with the music of Shahnaz
the Iranian virtuoso *tar* player
and just like that very first afternoon in the garden
something becomes more harmonious
as the music fills the space.
The image appears and grows on the white sheet
and at this moment as I watch and listen
a communion between the two
is taking place
between this music and this image.

Blue canvas

■ Far away unreachable mysterious
ever-changing forms
forests and flowers
birds and beasts
mountains
mansions
monuments
whole cities
searching
finding familiar forms in formlessness
discovering the joy of discovery
touching something mysterious
enchanting
beyond understanding
in the blue skies of my childhood.

A private intimate engagement
with somewhere so far away
and yet so much my own
perhaps my very first encounter with art
that mysterious field of human endeavour
that would become
my calling
my vocation.

The canvas:
blue
azure blue
cobalt blue
ultramarine blue
clear
sunny

star-studded
moonlit.

The medium:
textured clouds in the sky
shades of white and grey
hints of golden yellow
washes of all the nameless tints of red
burning
glowing
softening
dissolving
disappearing.

The tools:
my mind
my heart
the sense of sight
the seemingly endless world of a child's visual insight.

My role:
focus
find the forms
follow them
watch them evolve
emerge and erupt.
Be fast in perceiving a form
be willing to give it up
to another form emerging.
Surrender to an invisible hand
an invisible brush
creating with me this amazing

ephemeral imagery
learning the limits of my role
learning that the invisible hand on the brush
sometimes shows me monsters
when I try to find mountains to climb
and to see what is on the other side.

Later in life and in art
coming to terms with the limitations of my brush
the limitations of the forms I could create
in the face of the power of the invisible brush.
In the trials and tribulations of life and art
touching the abundance of possibilities
and freedoms within the boundaries
learning how to live life and how to create art
in the challenging
ineffable realm where surrender to the limits
and freedom to choose
both have a say
and the challenge is to find the invisible fluctuating
moving line that divides them
and to live in its vicinity.
At the start and the end of life
there is no choice but to surrender to what is given.
In the time between the two points
the forms and the freedoms are endless within the limits.

Just as on the blue canvas
in life too the forms have to be seen in the moment
appreciated and enjoyed
before they change and disappear.

Youth - detail

Watercolour
75 x 44 cm
2004
Private collection

Beyond the blue canvas

White jasmine flowers
spread on a neat and impeccable prayer rug
grandmother seated with a rosary in her raised hands
gazing at the blue sky above
whispering words I could not understand
communicating with a being whom I thought
resided beyond the blue canvas of the sky.

Our paternal grandmother
Bibi joon lived with us.
She lived to the age of ninety-eight
passed away when I was twenty-eight
when I had a four-month-old son.
Her love for our father and for us
was obvious in her deeds
in her ways of being
but seldom vocalized.

In those years her prayers were the focus of her life
and a mystery for me.
The scent of the jasmine flowers
the two layers of white embroidered cotton squares
on the colourful mat
the clay prayer stone
the colourful prayer beads
her small prayer books
her dedication and stillness
attracted me.
I sensed a certain beauty in her rituals
but was not sure if she loved
or feared the being beyond the blue sky
the focus of her regular frequent rituals.

Our father
a scientist and a humanist
never engaged in formal prayers.
He respected his mother's prayers and devotions
but his relationship to existence and life seemed different.
The focus of his dedication seemed to be near and tangible.
He believed in freedom
education and meaningful work.

His compassion was towards his family and friends.
He was loved and respected by all who knew him.
He left behind
a good name
and many good deeds.

Our mother prayed sometimes.
My sister and I prayed rarely
only when we had a hard exam.
No one ever criticized another
although *Bibi joon* liked to guide us to her way.

I now know how fortunate I was
to live and grow in this environment of freedom and acceptance
an environment of respect and no blind prejudice.
In the end we all went our own ways
left free to choose how we understood and related
with our inner and outer worlds.

Yet
I know nothing.
The darkest experience
forced me to search and ask

to cry and plead
and ask and search again.
I found no answer but surrender.

Empty faith everywhere
disappoints me
blind rituals
deeds contradicting words
words contradicting deeds
ruthless pursuit of power and personal gains
cloaked in sacred robes
depress and sadden me.
I walk away from it all
to the quiet solitude of my own unanswered questions.
The mystery remains.
The magnificence and complexities
of this limitless universe
are far beyond my comprehension.
The beauty
the order
the mystery
the indifference
fill me with awe
with wonder
and with disquiet.

Now the focus of my everyday life is here
wherever I am
and my aspiration
to live life responsibly.
Love
friendship

simplicity
nature and art
inspire and motivate me.
The limitless blue canvas of the sky
the scent of white jasmine flowers
still remind me of childhood innocence
and bring warmth to my heart.

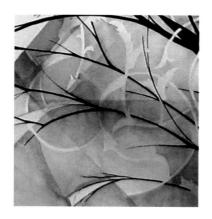

Green wall and red geraniums

■ It was a modest
brick house in Tehran
with a courtyard garden
and a high ivy-covered green wall.
This is the house in which I was born
in which I got married
and from which I left Iran to study in Europe.

With unrelenting resolve and passion
creativity and craftsmanship
my mother had set up
a little piece of paradise in the garden.
A water hose was guided up the green wall
attached to the top
to sprinkle the garden and transform the wall
into a vertical green waterfall
cooling the courtyard
in the hot summer evenings of Tehran.

This brick house
this green wall
this small courtyard
all this is vivid and present
in my memories of childhood days
still full of colour and feeling
after more than half a century.

Much of my childhood life was lived in the courtyard of
our three-story brick house in Tehran.

I see the high walls surrounding the courtyard
the large outdoor room

a room with the dome of the sky for a ceiling.

The heart of the courtyard
was a rectangular pool lined in blue tiles
surrounded by shrubs
and aromatic herbs
pansies and petunias planted in small
geometric flowerbeds.

I see the red goldfish
and the black and white one
swimming tirelessly in the pool.
I used to wonder if they slept at night.

I see the red geraniums
in earthen pots
their petals picked and arranged
carefully on our lips and nails
immersing us in hours
of imaginative joyful theatrical play.

Adults always seemed busy
benefitting from the fresh air and summer sunshine
planning and preparing for meals in the months ahead
while still keeping an eye on our adventures in the courtyard.

In the summer
green aromatic herbs were washed
chopped and spread to dry
on white sheets covering wooden beds.
For a few days
trays of tomato and pomegranate juice

were moved around the courtyard
following the path of the hot summer sunshine
turning into thick red sauces
their delicious unforgettable aroma filling the space.
Colourful jars of condiments and pickles
stood on windowsills
before being stored
in the cool basement cupboards.

From early spring to the start of autumn
we had breakfast and dinner
in the courtyard.
I can see the courtyard
swept and sprayed with water
in late afternoons.
I can smell the pleasant scent
rising from the hot wet brick
can see the wooden beds
covered with a rug or two
placed near the pool or by a tree
a few chairs and a table set up nearby.

In the late evenings
bundles of bedding
were opened and spread on the wooden beds
white mosquito nets suspended
lights turned out
and in the silence of the night
the moon and the stars witnessed
yet another transformation
of the busy courtyard into a large
open-air bedroom.

Sleeping in the courtyard
under the stars and the moon
waking up early under a blue sky
with the call of the rooster
and the rising of the sun
the murmur of the *samovar*
and the prospect of sweet tea
cheese and bread
are simple pleasures
remembered and cherished to this day.

Cycles of nature
the sun and the moon
the wind and the stars
water and vegetation
were interwoven with life in the courtyard house
an indigenous architecture
a life shared by many
families with the most modest means
those with wealth and all in between
benefitting from the well-being
of a harmonious connection
with the elements
sensible
sensitive
sustainable.

This is what I remember of life in the courtyard house
a way of life that has disappeared
a symbol of much deeper transformation
the congenial architecture of the courtyard house
taken over by concrete towers and grey skies

and red plastic geraniums in identical plastic pots
placed on stair landings
next to identical entrance doors
to identical apartments.

I have gone back.
Our courtyard house and others like it
have all vanished.

The architecture of many centuries
based on the rhythms of life of a people
their indigenous means and ways
their climate and culture
has disappeared
and in its place today
the architecture of concrete towers.
Towers with hearts of steel imposing their presence
on the people below
their only open space
the ramp to the underground parking garage
and two plastic cedars in two black pots
on the two sides of the metal gate
on the narrow pavement
and no green walls.

Garden of Oranges - detail

Watercolour, acrylic ink
102 x 66 cm
2012
Private collection

Of life and loss and pomegranate trees

■ Carefree summers
and short holidays throughout the year
were spent in a small garden in Isfahan.
I can see the garden
hear the sounds of life
touch and smell the flowers.
I can taste the sour cherries we picked from the trees
and the jam made from them.
It is my maternal grandmother's garden
the space in which
I first experienced the love of nature
the joy of togetherness and community.

Generations of extended family members
came together in this garden
grandmothers and great-aunts
our mother and aunts
joining hands to run the busy extended summer household
with laughter and stories
with song and dance
sometimes with whispers
tears and never ending talks
sometimes with sealed lips and secrets
but never with indifference.

Fruits were picked
jams and pickles made
meals served and stories told.
We experienced life in the garden
learnt from the elders the simple pleasures of life
the joy of community
hands and hearts coming together

to lift the heaviness of the household chores
and sometimes
the heaviness of the hearts.

Father only accompanied us
for a short period
in the three-month summer holiday
patiently supervising my sister and me
and a few cousins
writing and reading
reciting poetry
multiplication tables
riddles and puzzles
sometimes a composition to write
making sure we did not forget school
even though it was the summer holidays
and school seemed so far away.

With patience and calm
soft but serious words
love and caring
he instilled in us
the joy and the satisfaction of dedication to the work
that had to be done well
even in the midst of a carefree summer holiday.

The sounds
the scents
the sensations
the colours of this garden
are present in my memory
as soon as my mind goes back to those days.

On a very early summer morning
as darkness fades and daylight begins
I am half awake under the covers beneath the cool blue sky.
The rooster's song declares the start of another day.
The symphony of the birds takes over.
It is a serene and splendid moment
a dreamy and private moment with the mysterious
boundless beauty of the world.
How I have longed for that rooster's song.

Life starts early in the garden.
The seasons are all mixed up in my memory.
It is summer and spring
it is autumn
images and sensations
years and years overlapping.
I can smell the rose
the honeysuckle and the lilac
see the flowering pomegranate trees and the ripe pomegranates
the plum trees in blossom
the leafless persimmon trees heavy with fruit.
I can taste the sweet apricots
the sour cherries and the crisp apples.
I can taste the sour cherry jam spread on newly baked
warm buttered bread.
We are seated cross-legged
on a carpet on the raised *ayvan*
in a semi-circle around our maternal grandmother
the breakfast *sofreh* arranged in front of her
the *samovar* murmuring
the hot ashes in the *mangal* baking the eggs
and warming the bread on round copper plates.

I see the birds
the butterflies and the bees.

I remember the mosquito bites
and the familiar smell of the insect repellent *imshi*
sprayed through a hand-operated gadget
before the afternoon nap
in the rooms with white walls
high ceilings and niches
wood windows and white muslin curtains.

Even the sensation of the repulsive smell
of the weekly cleaning of the sewage wells
in the alleys beyond the garden wall
has remained in some corner of my memory.
We used to run away
from the overpowering odour
to the farthest corners of the garden
soon forgetting the smell
chasing a white butterfly
or playing hide and seek.

In this garden of many years and many memories
there is a pool lined with turquoise blue tiles
and filled with clear cool water
reflecting the sky.
Sometimes summer fruits
float on the surface of this blue cooler under the stars
and at festive times multi-coloured rose petals
and little white paper boats made
by small hands join
the fleet of fruits on the water.

Cool water rushes through the waterways.
From the fountain in the center
water rushes upwards and falls into the pool
then overflows
into the narrow irrigation ducts.

Where does all this water come from?
I remember asking
my maternal grandmother.
At the edge of the garden
just before the high mud-straw wall
a large raised structure
was shown to me
a reservoir full of water
with a few steps that led to the top.
The steps were never to be climbed
this was a forbidden place
a cruel giant lived at the bottom
and would draw in any child that came near.

Beyond the mud-straw walls of the garden
my grandmother showed me
the narrow rivulet
which branched out of the distant underground *qanat* system
also bringing water into the garden plots.

The picture and the terror of that dark structure
is as vivid in my mind
to this day
as the image of the shallow blue-tiled pool
full of joy and play
both containing the same water

one symbolic of terror
the other of joy.
I did not know then
that much later in life
a river on the other side of the planet
would bring back to me
the terror of the dark reservoir
a thousand fold
plunging me into the depth of
the most tragic unbearable event of my life.
This same river in which our son
was swimming with his friends
full of life and full of joy
took his life
moments later.

On that terror-filled day
standing on the rugged landscape of the island
on the shore of the river that took our son's life
the ruthlessness and the total indifference
of the same nature I had always felt close to
dawned on me.
This was the end.
I abhor this water and all waters for my remaining days.
And how do I now climb back up this rugged shore
to live life again after this?

At that moment of total despair
broken and shattered to my depth
with no desire or energy to make the climb
and continue living
just at that horror-filled moment

I looked up
the whole sky was suddenly covered with an image.
The face of our younger son filled the space
his eyes looking at me with a thousand questions
as if reading my mind and not believing what I was contemplating
an image full of love and grief
with a clear message
which made me shiver and cry to my depth.

I had no choice in this.
Our sixteen-year-old son
whom we had left standing
in tears and confusion
on the street in front of the house
as we rushed to the accident site several hours away
was telling me what I had to do
to take the first
heavy and broken mournful step
with a stooped back and aching heart
and begin the climb up the rugged shore of the river
to the road that would take us back to a totally altered life.

I had to accept and surrender
to the unthinkable pain of this greatest loss
learn to live a different existence
learn to feel and cherish all the care and love
that surrounds me
as I struggle to make sense
of my life and my new reality.

Nineteen years later
now a grandmother with love and happiness in my heart

living on the shores of the Pacific Ocean
I reminisce about life
joy and pain
still visit the gardens in my memory
the joys of the blue pool
and the terror of the black reservoir.
And I still paint
memories of pomegranate trees
and blue pools of water
pondering the unpredictable
turbulence and turmoil of a life
and the unexpected resilience and tolerance
that evolves with time.

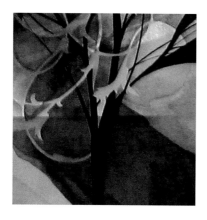

Expressing the inexpressible

■ A year has passed
the agony has not.

Overwhelmed with grief and sadness
I am walking on a quiet beach
listening through earphones
to the music played and sang
by an Iranian musician who has asked me to create a painting
for the cover of his first album.

It is a powerful experience to be with this music
in this landscape
the rebirth of nature happening all around me.
I have the same questions as those the artist is posing
and feel the longing for an answer in the depth of my being
as I have known and am going through
the pain of a great loss.

It is not only the words and the voice that speak
it is the language of the music that communicates and conveys.
I hear and feel the yearning
the knocking
the restless walking
the searching
the asking
the begging.

I hear the quest
the inevitable quest
the indefinable quest of our experience as humans.

Then there is the pause

the quiet contemplation
the expectation and joy of a discovery.
The equanimous voice of wisdom follows
surrender
thoughtfulness
emptiness
the void.

The words echo the message.
Only if you give up everything
and sacrifice the self to the last strand of hair
are you liberated and allowed entry.
There is an awareness of this moment and the restless pain
of search and yearning
give way to the discovery of this magnificent
and ephemeral moment of life
that has to be lived with joy.
This music is powerful and healing
as it inspires transcending the tragic
and embracing the full experience of living.

At this moment
I realize how hard it will be for me
to express this richness of meaning
on a sheet of paper
to be reproduced as the artwork for the cover of the album.

I look up.
The branches of a magnificent tree are over my head
each branch with its new green buds
reaching outwards to the light like outstretched hands
as if joining the musician in his quest.

The branches form an intricate lattice over my head
through which I see the dome of the pale blue sky
alluding perhaps to another realm
to which this music can be a door.

Under my feet is the earth
and the music seems to connect the two.

The visual language starts to take form
the door
which has to be found and opened.
The square
the symbol of the earth and the experience of finite existence.
The circle
the symbol of the spiritual realm.
The lattice of the foliage
as the veil that has to be penetrated in the search
and the seven stations of love
that have to be crossed
to reach the pure emptiness and peace
of the void within
and the sense of connection to a greater reality.

I am aware of the limitations of
attempting to portray this music
and the thoughts and feelings it conveys.

A visual expression can perhaps capture
only one moment of the experience.
For expressing the inexpressible
as Aldous Huxley has stated
nothing matches the music.

Radiance

Watercolour, acrylic ink
100 x 74 cm
2008
Private collection

A collage of many gardens

■ I see a multi-layered mesh of
sinuous
silken
intricately woven blossoms
floating over the tree trunks
beneath the ever blue sky.

I see the jewel-like golden yellow plums
translucent and sweet
caressed by the clusters of green leaves
in summer sunshine
or leafless branches
heavy with gatherings of orange persimmons
on an autumn day.

Layers of images of vibrant gardens
full of colour and life
memories from a faraway childhood
mingle with more recent images
images gathered on my trips back
images of grieving gardens
in the grip of a heartless greedy season
the trees uprooted in the darkness of the night
their networks of roots
replaced by systems of steel rods
their trunks by steel columns.

I ask myself if the vibrant garden exists
anywhere but in my imagination
this persistent garden that I find myself in
whenever I am in nature
anywhere in the world

reminiscing and comparing
this garden that I have painted in the studio
and exhibited on gallery walls for so many years.

Perhaps the garden in my memories
is not one garden
but a collage of many
of many courtyard gardens of my childhood
our house in Tehran
grandmother's garden in Isfahan
or the one in which my great-grandmother
lived with her son and his family.

Perhaps it is in a village
or by the side of a road in the vast dry desert.
It is attached to the one-room coffee houses
on the routes between the cities we travelled to
in a bus or in a car
the mud-brick walled space
the oasis with one tree and a small pool
and two geranium plants
growing eagerly out of the dry cracked soil
in the two earthen pots by the pool.

My garden is perhaps a collage of many grand
monumental Persian gardens
visited in the span of many years
that have come together
in layers and layers
of transparent timeless time
and placeless place
in the mysterious realm of my creative imagination.

It could be the ancient Pasargadae garden
of which few fragments of the foundations remain
near the modest tomb of Cyrus the Great
a garden from twenty-five hundred years before
the same once magnificent garden
a model for the later Chahar Bagh gardens
all over the world.

It is a garden in a city
one of many
disappearing
one by one
in Tehran
in Isfahan or in Shiraz
in Yazd or in Mashhad
being pushed out of existence through
the insatiable thirst for more.
It is a geometrically ordered space
an ancient archetype and a universal symbol
an oasis of cool green shade and narrow blue waterways
a manifestation of the poetic approach to nature
shared by Iranians from prehistory to the present.

It is a garden walled and protected
from the dusty desert of yesterday
and the noise and confusion of car traffic of today.

It is perhaps the Garden of Eram
in the city of Shiraz.
I have walked quietly in meditation
over the symmetrical geometric layout of its pathways
bathed my eyes in the cool blue water

of the large rectangular pool
in front of its main pavilion
followed the narrow long waterways
flowing out to irrigate
groves of orange trees
the tall slender cedar trees
the famous *sarv-e-naz* of Shiraz.
I have breathed in the sweet scent
of its many coloured roses.

The sights and sensations
have never left me
the coolness under the shade of the trees
the sparkle of the blue in the pools
the scent of the orange blossoms.

The garden of my memories
could also be the one surrounding the tomb of Hafez in Shiraz
the tomb of the beloved poet of all Persians
where masses of paper-thin
pink bougainvillea in large earthen pots
line the walkways
towards the simple open pavilion
encircling his marble tomb.
In one unforgettable visit
barefoot long before reaching the marble steps
my heart filled with joy and sorrow
my face pressed on his cool tombstone
as I wept bitterly
for the complicated
yet simple beauty and melancholy of life
portrayed so timelessly in his poems.

The images overlap
fade and find a focus again
on the great long pool in the Dowlatabad Garden
in the ancient desert city of Yazd.
By the pool I see young female university students
in black robes and scarves
with large sketchbooks
sitting on the wide wooden *kelim* covered benches
absorbed in sketching the brick pavilion near the pool.
Some look up and smile
as I move closer
curious to see their sketches.
I am taken back almost fifty years
to a similar space
but a very different scene
sketching with a mixed group of classmates
in colourful clothing
all of us from the architectural school.

The image changes again.
It is the Garden of Fin in Kashan
with its delightful open pavilions
and waterways running through the buildings
out into the gardens
where in the midst of the utmost refinement and beauty
horrendous historical events took place
in the last century
the thoughts of which always darken and tarnish
the experience of my frequent visits there.
Despite this the order and the beauty attracts me
and timeless elements of this garden
have found their way into my paintings.

This collage of gardens
full of colour and life and vitality
is alive in my memories and my imagination.

Now each time I go back
another of the old private urban gardens
has been taken over
by our twenty-first century inexhaustible greed.
Instead of living trees and green foliage
tall steel columns and cranes
rise above the old mud-brick walls
soon to be replaced by shiny granite walls.

In disappointment I wonder and ask
why is it that these spaces of serenity and beauty
are losing their vital role in the life of a people
and in the urban fabric of Iranian cities?

The female architect I met on a trip to Kashan
who devoted seven years of her life
to preserving and recreating the beauty and serenity
of a three-hundred year old courtyard house
answers my question:

> Our worldview has changed
> from the desire to live better lives
> to the goal of making more money
> and that is why we are demolishing
> beautiful serene and green gardens
> and courtyard houses
> to create in their place
> concrete towers.

It is not the quality of lives
lived in these new homes that is important.
It is the amount of money
gained through this transformation that matters.

These green spaces of tranquility and beauty
the Persian courtyard houses
and gardens that thrived throughout centuries
will only endure in a few garden-museums
in books and photographs
and memories
the special quality of life experience within these spaces
lost with the demise of our aging generation.

Living museums
such as the house in Kashan
will give a few fortunate individuals
who may for a few days pass through them
a hint of the life of centuries past
a hint of spaces planned and inhabited
over many centuries
on the basis of a thoughtful
sustainable and respectful relationship with nature.

Blue Butterfly

Watercolour, acrylic ink
40 x 60 cm
2012
Private collection

Sour cherry jam

■ Sour cherry trees
at the furthest end of the garden
narrow unpaved walkways
dark red cherries
white butterflies
the buzzing sound
of insects
not seen but heard
the afternoon sun
heat vibrating in front of my eyes
no sound from the grown-ups taking an afternoon nap
far away in the building
at the other end of the garden.

I am back in time
on a mid-summer vacation
in our maternal grandmother's garden in Isfahan.

With my sister
three younger half-cousins
our youngest aunt and uncle
close in age and spirit
we have decided to have an afternoon
tea party at this end of the garden.
We are going to pick sour cherries from the trees
start a small fire
set up our metal tripod
put our small copper pan on top
add the picked cherries
to the cup of sugar in the pan
and make sour cherry jam
to eat with bread for our afternoon picnic.

The youngest of us
perhaps three years old
the oldest our uncle thirteen
and I six years old
a bond of love and caring between us
stronger than the rivalry and disagreements of childhood play.

We are running around
gathering thin dry branches
piling them up
watching with anticipation and excitement
as our uncle starts the fire.
Can he do it?
Will it work?

The sight and smell of smoke rising up
the sensation on my face
of the heat from the small fire
at the centre of our gathering
the burning eyes and tears
the joy and laughter
have remained with me
the taste of that hot sweet jam on bread
never forgotten.

Perhaps we were all experiencing
in our innocent play
a new sense of freedom
of daring and adventure
being present in that exciting moment
a first time experience
a sense of togetherness.

We were feeling the camaraderie and conviviality
of working together for something worthwhile
a sweet outcome in the end.

And so the image and the memory
of that first cooking adventure
the taste of that sour cherry jam
made in a circle of friendship and joy
remains sweet and strong to this day.

Perhaps my lifelong interest in cooking
started in that small pot of sour cherry jam
in our intimate and open kitchen
under the boundless sky.

Monarch Butterfly

Watercolour, acrylic ink
53 x 43 cm
2006
Private collection

In our father's library

A room overflowing with books
on the second floor
of the courtyard house in Tehran
has a special place in the memories of my childhood years.
This room was our father's library.

It had two tall windows
overlooking the courtyard and the small blue pool.
The windows had thick textured curtains
beige background and navy blue motifs
sewn by our mother
her creative touch always present in every room of this house.

The other three walls were lined
with brown wooden bookshelves
almost up to the ceiling.
More books were piled on the large brown wooden desk
sometimes on the two armchairs
and on the table beside them
books in Persian
in English and French
in Arabic
and it seemed books on every subject.
Books on various fields of medical science and genetics
our father's field of study
occupied one tall bookshelf.
But books on
history
literature
fine arts
even cookbooks and children's books
all had a place on these shelves.

Before we could read
my sister and I were permitted to explore
heavy volumes of books
with hundreds of colourful pictures of birds and fish
flowers and trees
mammals and human figures
complicated anatomical drawings.
I can still feel the heaviness of those books
see the glossy pages
sometimes turning yellow at the edge.
Other volumes had maps and pictures
of cities and buildings
carpets and paintings.
An amazing universe was out there
and how exciting to get a glimpse
of all those faraway wonders on the pages of these books
on the shelves of this room
on the second floor of the courtyard house.

With reading came a whole new experience
unmatched by any other.
I was in awe
of how many books on how many different subjects
our father had collected in this library.
The thought of all the knowledge
in those books
and the people who wrote them
made me feel small and insignificant.
Had our father read all those books?
I remember wondering if I could ever read
so many books in my life
and what if I couldn't?

The heaviness of the task
and the seeming impossibility
of accomplishing such a task saddened me.

Eventually I realized that I could not
and would not read all those books.
But soon books filled an important part of my life.
These silent books took me to places
beyond the four walls of the room
to faraway places
and bygone times
to places filled with mystery
with poetry and adventure.
This is the room I liked the most in the house
the room that instilled in me the love of reading.

The image is vivid
our father working behind the desk
standing immersed in his thoughts
in front of a bookshelf or reading and dozing off in an armchair.
We could all be with him in this room
if we kept quiet.
Somehow the room
his quiet presence
and the rows of books on the shelves
inspired in us calmness and curiosity at the same time.
A picture is etched in my memory
lying on the floor under the desk
at a very young age with my sister
each of us absorbed in a book
for what seemed like endless time
our father reading or writing on the desk above.

When we were older we would bring our homework
talk about school
receive a special piece of blotting paper
a pencil or a pen or a book
a prize for an achievement at school.

From his trip to India
our father brought back a bust of Mahatma Gandhi
and a live green parrot in a cage.
They were both given a warm and excited welcome
and a special place in the library.
The green parrot in the cage
with its red and blue bands of feathers
around the neck transformed the room
bringing a hint of the green freedom of the forest
to the heavy warm brown and blue colours of the room.
But alas
to our disappointment
the parrot did not speak
turned inwards and remained silent.
Within a day or two
coming from the heat of India
to the cold winter of Tehran
the green parrot perished and left us.
Astonished and saddened
my sister and I wanted to know why.
Perhaps it missed its homeland we were told.

The bust of Mahatma
was more robust and lived
in a place of much respect
on the bookshelf for many years.

We heard from our father
the amazing story of the man Gandhi was
his life's work and his dedication to his cause.
Our father admired Mahatma Gandhi
the respect and esteem he held for him
apparent in his words about him.
The bust moved with our parents
to another house in Tehran
was placed on another bookshelf
in the new library for several more years
silently witnessing the changing
evolving life in the library
in the house and in the city
in the whole country
witnessing the upheavals
uncertainties and confusions
until the day when finally
the family decision was made to leave Iran.

In those days of questions and confusions
about unknown futures and hard choices
the bust of Mahatma Gandhi did not make
the trip to Vancouver with our family.
The books on Persian literature and poetry
were packed into boxes to travel thousands of miles
in buses and trains and a ship
to join us on the shores of the Pacific Ocean
pieces of a cherished heritage
we needed for support in a new chosen home
symbolic foundations
for new multi-layered identities.

Knowing that a phase in his life had passed
our father parted with his books on science.
The books found a new home in a university library in Isfahan
the city where our father was born.

The fate of Mahatma Gandhi's bust
is lost in my memory now and I have no one to ask
but its symbolic presence and meaning persist to this day
belief in justice and freedom
dedication and selflessness
perseverance and sincerity
can achieve the seemingly unachievable.

A Persian library on the shores of a sea

The most cherished of his belongings
travelled with him in cardboard boxes
bound souvenirs from the country he had left behind.
Books of Persian poetry and literature
books of history and art
came with our father
to his new home in Vancouver
and found their place on bookshelves
in a small room with a desk and a chair
his sanctuary
where he spent endless hours
of the last twenty-five years of his life.

I see him in his woollen cardigan
under the light of a table lamp
a large magnifying glass in his hand
quiet and focused
absorbed in a book for hours.

Concerned and sad about the events in Iran
he immersed himself
in the wisdom and the beauty of thought and language
within the covers of those books
treasures that could not be taken away from him
the heritage that kept him connected
to a place he had loved and had left.

I see him copying a poem
in his neat and delicate handwriting
in small notebooks and pieces of paper.
I see him seated in front of a computer
trying patiently to learn the new skill.

Young at heart
he did not want to be left behind.

He was already dreaming
of bringing a cherished part of his culture to his new home
thinking of books of poetry and literature
history and art
not just for himself and his family
but for the larger family of Iranians
who had now become Iranian-Canadians
newcomers who needed to remember
and continue to cherish the old
in order to be able to respect and cherish the new.

Settling down in West Vancouver
our father transported
the spirit of his library in Tehran
to the neighbourhood public library
spending the last twenty years of his life
painstakingly fundraising
ordering and cataloguing
creating a Persian collection
for the thousands of Iranians in Vancouver.
Our children should not forget
the culture and the language
he used to say.

I remember from a very young age hearing from him
about the beauty and the wisdom of this culture
but also about disregard and insensitivity to culture
the problems that have to be recognized
have to be addressed.

For him education and books were
instruments for eradication of ignorance
and attaining a better life.

With his dedication to creating
the Persian Collection for the library
when he was an octogenarian
he demonstrated
not with his words
but with his deeds
his love of books and learning.

In those years
full of despair and confusion
for the uprooted Iranians now settled
on the shores of this great ocean
his unrelenting focus and devotion
to the creation of the collection was inspiring.

The Persian books on the shelves
of the West Vancouver Memorial Library
remind us of the positive elements of our heritage
encourage us to persevere despite the hardship.
The books bring us together through poetry
through literature and art
until we gradually can stand again
and build new lives
new identities
enriched by the blending of our two cultures.

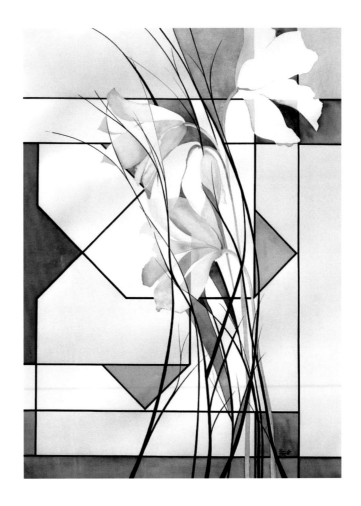

Abstraction and Resemblance

Watercolour, acrylic ink
100 x 72 cm
2008
Private collection

A room of our own

The room had only three walls.
The sloped ceiling came down to the floor on one side.
Two identical triangles formed two parallel walls.
The third wall
a rectangle
had a door in the middle
almost one meter high and about half a meter wide.
A ceiling light hung a few centimeters down from the ceiling.

This was our special room under the stairs
that my younger sister and I
had the fortune to discover
decorate and enjoy
for many hours of the day
our special doll house
beneath the staircase
in the house of our childhood.

Our mother
an expert in making a silk purse out of a sow's ear
helped us turn this space under the stairs
into a little doll house.
The creation of the doll house
when she was in her late twenties
was perhaps as much fun for her as for us.

On one of the triangular walls
she had hung a small curtain
alluding to a window behind it.
A small rug covered the floor.
On the side where the ceiling met the floor
we stacked shoeboxes for shelves and beds for the dolls.

Our mother had a passion for sewing
and the remnants from sewing our clothes
became the material
for making the dolls
and soft furnishings for the doll house.

My sister and I
and one or even two little friends
could just manage to sit on the floor of this house
if the door was kept open
and one of us agreed to be
half in and half out.
Little friends who lived in more spacious houses
liked to visit the doll house
under the stairs
and asked their parents for a similar place.

Our mother was our first mentor
igniting the creative spark
inspiring us to design and build
our imagined worlds.

Both my sister and I studied architecture
and later devoted our adult lives to
creative endeavours.

T-squares and triangles

▌ Tens and tens of sketches
of Venus and Hercules
sheets of paper and notebooks dedicated to
drawing views of hexahedrons and polyhedrons
intersecting spheres and cylinders
notebooks filled with problems and solutions
to abstract mathematical problems
pots of black tea
sleepless nights
anxious days and entrance exams.

Now hardly breathing
I am standing in front of the
entrance gates of Tehran University.

Hundreds and hundreds of names
printed on large sheets of paper
pasted upon a board
by the entrance gates
students struggling to get close
eyes racing over the printed rows
futures seemingly determined
on these lists.
Finally I see
my name on three lists
architecture
English literature
mechanical engineering.

A weight has lifted.

I will be an architect.

At the end of the first school week
wearing the compulsory long dark grey robe
over my clothes
I am given a drafting table
and a tall narrow metal cabinet
both old and spattered with
different colours of ink and paint.
The cabinet
I fill with tools
T-squares and triangles
pens and pencils
a roll of tracing paper
and pots of ink.

Fifty years later
I still have unsettling dreams
seeing myself standing in front of the open door
of the narrow metal cabinet
looking inside
anxious and fearful
not knowing what I have to do.

It was 1964.
There were two schools of architecture in Iran.
We were six girls in a class of sixty students.
Now in 2015 there are seven hundred schools of architecture in Iran
more than half the students are female.
The statistics are impressive
the picture more complex.
Much has changed in these fifty years.

We make detailed renditions of Greek temples.

We study and draw Doric
Ionic and Corinthian columns.
We study Tuscan and Composite columns of
the Roman Architectural Orders.
I see the harmony of the proportions
the beauty of the details
but still it all seems distant and unfamiliar.
The study of Persian architecture
its masterpieces and its elements of design
would come later.
My spirit soars with the study
of those familiar spaces
where life had been lived by
generations of my ancestors
over hundreds of years.

We are in the studio
gathering around a large table created
by pulling several tables together
the professor sitting at the head
all of us from the newest freshmen
to the graduating class
surrounding him
awaiting his comments about our attempts at designing
a house
a school
an auditorium
and sometimes a whole neighbourhood.

We were encouraged to discover the true beauty
of the vernacular art and architecture of Iran.
We studied old towns of centuries before

learnt how the philosophy and way of life
the natural environment
building materials and technologies
and the artistic and poetic sensibilities
of a people had come together
to create masterpieces of architecture
over several centuries
many now listed on the UNESCO world heritage documents.

We were intent on using
those sensibilities
those concepts and architectural elements in our projects
modernizing them for life in the twentieth century
naively thinking that architecture alone
could bring positive change
to people's lives.

It is 1976.
Since graduation from the school of architecture
my further studies in England
and my return to Iran
I have worked in urban development planning
in a government organization
and in a small private architectural firm.
I have gained some experience.

I have now started working on an inspiring project.

There are fifteen of us architects and urban planners
in the architectural department
of a large consulting firm in Tehran
working on the design of a small new town

for a textile factory in an industrial complex
in south-eastern Iran.
We have visited the existing nearby towns
photographed and sketched
the traditional layouts
the architectural elements
have interviewed potential future residents
have sat with them
in their destitute dwellings of cardboard and rags
asked about their lives
their needs and aspirations
realizing how little we truly know and understand
self conscious of our limitations
but still intoxicated with the thought and the possibility
of changing many lives for the better
through appropriate architectural and urban design.

We have surveyed the topography
and the natural elements of the site.
We have studied the path of the sun
the direction of the wind.
We have discussed the needs
the possibilities
the spirit and feeling of the town
the intended living environment and conditions
the costs and technologies.
We have sketched
drawn master plans and detailed drawings.
We have made models.
We have resisted proposals of co-operation
from the keen consultants beyond the borders of Iran.
This is to be our project.

It is to be inspired by the traditional architecture of Iran
suited to the environment and the climate
and the needs of the future inhabitants
but built for life in the twentieth century and beyond.

We are committed to this
have many hopes and many dreams.

In the midst of the design process
the revolution happens.
Everything changes
the people
the language
the priorities.
The project is postponed.
Within a short time the war with Iraq is raging.
The traditional cities of the south
our sources of inspiration
are being bombed.
Innocent people perish
buildings of bygone centuries turning to dust.

Our second son is born in the winter of 1980
in the maternity ward of a Tehran hospital as the city is being bombed.
He spends his first night on my bed
in a hospital blacked-out for protection against bombing.

I find myself questioning everything
our dreams and aspirations
goals and responsibilities.
I become painfully aware of the limits of architecture
in inspiring and bringing about true change in anyone's life.

That naïve hope has been lost
with so much more
in these times of contradictions and confusions.
Fearful of the outcome of war
we give up.
Sad and confused about the events taking place
anxious about the future of our children
we finally leave Iran.

The departure from Iran
was for me
also a departure from the profession.
Although I still tried and managed
to continue with the work for some years
in a new and totally different environment
the spirit and passion were missing for me.

In the seclusion
of an art studio
in the basement of our new home in Vancouver
I begin to paint memories
of the urban spaces threatened by war
and the Persian gardens of my childhood.
Immersed in the poetry and music
of the land and the dreams left behind
I paint the spirit
of those lost environments
on sheets of paper
in vivid happy colours
that had disappeared
from life in that beloved distant place.
It is for me a way to stay connected.

The young students of architecture in Iran
in the twenty-first century
still visit the Persian architectural masterpieces
that have survived the centuries
the repeated earthquakes and the wars.
They sketch and photograph
and write essays about them.
But they seem to have lost
the reverence we had for those spaces.
Their eyes are focused on the wider world
and what the new concepts
technologies and materials make possible.

The works of nameless
master architects and builders of their ancestral heritage
do not seem to truly inspire them.

Their idols in architecture
reside and work in large multinational firms
in affluent metropolitan centres.
The projects they aspire to and celebrate
rise up to the sky
in unfamiliar increasingly absurd forms
designed and built
for those who endlessly search for everything new
and have the financial means to experiment with
and experience such novelties.
The majority of the human populations of the world
are left behind to search for their own solutions
in the shanty towns of the world
in the fringes of war-torn cities
in uncaring sprawling squalid suburbs.

To learn from the spirit and philosophy
of those traditional urban spaces and architectural elements
to learn from their simplicity
their sustainability and their harmony
and to create a contemporary architecture
for the twenty-first century
based on those principals
needs conviction and support
from the powers and sources
that shape a society.

Will this happen one day
I ask myself
unwilling to give in
to the negative hopeless response
that seems to be the answer to such questions.

For me at this time and in this place
T-squares and triangles
pencils and paints
are tools to create
imagined gardens and architectural spaces
inspired by the poetry of Persian poets
on sheets of white paper in a studio
thousands of miles away from
the school of architecture
that taught me how to use these tools
for the design of real buildings and architectural spaces.
I now have modest goals
have chosen to create these imagined spaces
on paper to keep my connection
with those cherished monuments and disappearing spaces.

Pomegranate Tree and Window - detail

Watercolour, acrylic ink
125 x 66 cm
2010
Artist's collection

A winter celebration

■ In the house of my childhood
the last month of autumn
and the approaching cold winter nights
brought the promise of the *korsi*.
It was installed every year in *Bibi joon's* room
the setting up
an important ritual
with much excitement.
For *Bibi joon*
our paternal grandmother
the *korsi* had a special meaning and significance.
It was her *korsi*
would be set up with her taste and her instructions
and would bring the family
to her room for warmth and togetherness
during the winter months.

A low square table
measuring about one meter on each side
was set up over the carpet
in the middle of *Bibi joon's* room.
A thick sheet protected the carpet.
The *mangal*
a metal brazier for hot coal
was placed in the centre of a round copper tray
on the thick sheet under the table.
Large cotton-filled *toshaks*
the size of a thin mattress and covered with white sheets
were placed on the carpet on the four sides of the table.
Three very large and thick cushions
rested on three walls providing back support.
The fourth *toshak* facing the door had no back support.

A very large white sheet
about five meters on each side
was spread on top of the table
overlaid with a thick and warm
square quilt measuring about four meters on each side
dropping over the mattresses
covering them completely.
Over this quilt a smaller
embroidered and colourful cloth would be spread
with a round engraved copper tray
placed in the centre.

Bibi joon kept the *korsi* very tidy and clean.
The room was aired all the time
the sheets washed and ironed every two weeks
the engraved copper tray dusted and polished
the small bowls of nuts and candy
or pomegranates and sweet lemons
replenished every few days.

The experience was worth the hard work.

This was the room we would
gather in on weekends and holidays
and on winter days after school
from late afternoon
until bedtime
sitting on the futons
with feet out-stretched under the warm *korsi*
the quilt covering our bodies
our heads and shoulders
exposed to the cool fresh air of the room.

Homework
family gatherings and conversations
reading of books and poetry
newspapers and crossword puzzles
backgammon games
eating of meals
all happened around this *korsi*
during the winter months.
A large wooden radio
stood on a small chest of drawers
and entertained us with music
poetry recitations and the evening news
or the *'Story of the Night'*
a program of stories read from world literature.

The winter festival *Shab-e-Yalda* was celebrated
around *Bibi joon's korsi*
on the longest and darkest night of the year
occurring on the Northern Hemisphere's winter solstice.
Memories of family gatherings on those nights
bring back feelings of warmth and excitement
eating watermelons
sweet and sour pomegranates
dried nuts and fruits
listening to winter stories
readings of Hafez poetry
games and laughter until midnight
and going to bed with the promise
of longer days and shorter nights.

These simple gatherings have remained with me
amongst the most cherished memories of my life.

Pomegranates

Watercolour, acrylic
75 x 32 cm
2004
Private collection

Celebration of Nowruz

■ It happened every year.
One winter day
when the sun was shining a little warmer
and we had left for school
without a warm hat or a heavy coat
we would come home
and see carpets being cleaned in the courtyard
adults too busy to notice us
and we knew lunch would be simple and fast.

Our family was getting ready for Nowruz festivities
like all Iranian families who had
for centuries
celebrated the arrival of spring and the New Year
with special rituals.

The air was warmer
a surge of green buds
were suddenly visible on the trees
the birds sounded more cheerful.
It was as if like us
the whole of nature
was in anticipation of a joyous event.

We would run inside the house
in the carpetless
curtainless rooms
and hear our voices echoed back
the windows open
and the *korsi* in *Bibi joon*'s room dismantled.
The yearly custom of spring-cleaning
before the arrival of Nowruz had started.

Coming back from school
a new surprise awaited us everyday.

The small blue-tiled pool was cleaned
filled with fresh water and red gold fish
and colourful pansies were planted in narrow plots around the pool.

Our new dresses
sewn by our mother
were ready to be tried on
together with the new black and shiny patent shoes
and white socks.

For a few days the house filled with female relatives
to help with baking of Nowruz cookies and candies.
Like a small candy and pastry factory
the aroma of rosewater and cardamom
saffron and cinnamon
greeted us in the street
before we entered the narrow alleyway and the courtyard.
Our favourite chore was arranging
the small traditional cookies
in tins and boxes
tasting everything
trying to decide which was the most delicious.

The yearly rituals of preparations for Nowruz
the excitement and anticipation
never became routine.
There was always novelty
and surprises that occurred
within the context of traditions of centuries before.

About ten days before the first day of spring
lentils and grains of wheat were soaked in water
for making a plate of green sprouted grains
symbolizing rebirth in nature.
The sprouts were spread on plates
sprinkled with water everyday
growing to a green living tuft
ready to be displayed as part of the *Sofreh-ye haft sin*.

My favourite project
was the painting of the eggs for the Nowruz spread.
The supplies were small pieces of printed colourful fabrics
onion skins and coloured inks
a few small paint brushes
and one dozen eggs.
Our project was to complete the painting of the eggs
previously covered and tied with onions skins
or pieces of printed fabrics
and boiled in water
the pastel colour of the red onion skins
and the faint patterns of the printed fabrics
already visible on them
ready for our creative marks.

The night before Nowruz
the special spread, *Sofreh-ye haft sin*
was set up in our home
by our mother with everyone's help
just as in every Iranian home
the culmination of a month of preparations
for the festivities and rituals rooted in traditions
from more than two thousand years before.

Seven items symbolizing
love and light
rebirth and fertility
health and beauty
patience and affluence
their names starting with the letter *sin* or s
were arranged on plates and set on
the table on a special cloth.

A mirror and flowers
a red goldfish in a bowl
coloured eggs and candles
an orange floating in a bowl of water
and several small plates of special Nowruz cookies
completed the *Sofreh-ye haft sin*.

The exact moment the sun crosses the celestial equator
usually around March 21st
marks the beginning of spring
when the length of day and night are exactly the same
and when the old year ends
and the New Year begins.

Every year our family gathered around the *sofreh*
awaiting the special moment
when the old year ended and the New Year began
even if it happened during the night.

The images of many spreads over the years
are all mixed up and hazy in my memory
but some moments and sensations remain
vivid and present to this day.

The fragrance of the pot of flowering hyacinth
the image and scent of the branches of
the Persian ice flower
the goldfish
the coloured eggs
the taste of the crunchy almond and honey brittles
all come back to me
my body awakened to the delicious sensations.

I see *Bibi joon* seated in front of the *sofreh*
dressed in a green and dark red
paisley-patterned jacket
her coloured dark brown hair neatly combed and parted in the middle
covered with a thin white scarf
held tight with a small decorative pin under her chin
silently reading the Qur'an.
I savour the faint scent of rose water
as I hug her and kiss her soft wrinkled cheeks.

I see our father and mother
dressed elegantly
father in a suit and tie
mother in a dress she has sewn herself
my sister and me in new dresses and shoes
excited and awaiting our gifts of green and red bills
with the special smell of new money.

Since *Bibi joon* was the eldest member of our extended family
every relative and friend living in Tehran
would pay a visit to our house
starting very shortly after the moment
that marked the arrival of the New Year.

I remember so many occasions
when we still had not finished the special New Year meal
of fried or smoked fish and saffron and herb rice
when the door bell would ring
and groups of visitors would arrive
with their joyful greetings and wishes.
The visits were just for a cup of tea and a few home-baked cookies
praised as the best every year.

During the first twelve days of the New Year
every relative and friend would visit our home.
Father wrote everyone's name on a list
making sure that our family would return all the visits
during these same twelve days.
The visits made possible
new beginnings
more warmth and closeness
in relationships and friendships
even the ones that had grown cold
in the previous twelve months.

The thirteenth day of the New Year
was celebrated with a picnic
sizdah-be-dar in the fresh spring air
in a garden or a green field outside the city.
We children both loved and dreaded this day.
It was a happy day of games and sports
good food and much laughter
with many extended family members
but also a day of making sure
all our homework was finished and ready
for school the next day.

The memory of sitting or lying on a blanket
in the shade of a tree
under the blue sky
with an open exercise book
a pen and an ink pot in front of me
copying verses of Sa'di
or a passage from the text book
has remained with me
together with the hint of a silent feeling of regret
for not having finished this work
in the previous twelve days.

Years later away from Iran
we celebrated every Nowruz with our aging parents
preserving the beautiful rituals and traditions.
Now after their depart
we continue the celebration
transferring the elements of these traditions
to our children and grandchildren.
Our move and new life in Vancouver
home to many people from all corners of the world
has given us the opportunity to
participate in and enjoy
many more celebrations and festivals.
Life is richer and more meaningful
when we understand and share
each other's happy moments and joyous events.

Separation

Watercolour
72 x 50 cm
2004
Private collection

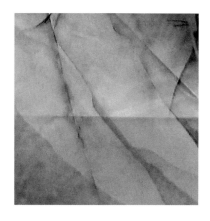

Joy of poetry

■ Warm summer evenings
a table and a few chairs on the brick-paved courtyard
and some nights
more chairs and more people.

On the table
plates of green grapes and cucumbers
a pitcher of ice-cold *sekanjebin* and glasses
and a few books
neatly covered with brown paper
or old newspaper.

The language spoken here
is not the same as the ordinary language
of everyday speech.
Each person
perhaps my mother
my grandmother
a friend or a relative
taking their time
to ponder and utter words and phrases
which sound like soft lullabies.
The next one
perhaps my father
or another relative responding immediately
or sometimes
taking more time
and more
to finally express his response
a formal recitation
sounding like a song
a piece of music.

Everyone is now clapping in admiration
for what was expressed
a line not known by many
but beautiful and profound.

I would look and listen
wide-eyed
curious and excited
sensing the special joy and contentment
that filled the space and appeared as smiles
on the faces of these people whom I loved.

Now and then there is a dispute
and one of the books is consulted
discussions take place
about proper pronunciations
or meanings
and soon the dispute is resolved
the magical conversation is resumed again
going around the circle
everyone reciting his or her piece.

As the moon and the stars appear in the sky above
lights are turned on
illuminating the faces of the people around the table
and leaving the surrounding trees and shrubs
in a mysterious semi-darkness.

The music of the language spoken in that mysterious light
was always mesmerizing
even if the meanings were far from accessible for me
at that young age.

Most nights my younger sister and I
sitting or lying on the carpet covered wooden beds nearby
listening to these poetic exchanges
would struggle against falling asleep
counting the stars
eyes following the movement of the clouds
and the moon
in the deep dark-blue sky above
absorbing the poems being recited.

In time
we learnt the rules of this game of poetry
or *moshaereh*
a line of poetry recited from memory
by one participant
and then silence
waiting for a response
the next participant searching for a line
beginning with the letter ending the last word
of the previously recited line.
A face lights up and the triumphant
participant recites the suitable line of poetry
which has come to the surface
from the depth of the mysterious depository
of memory where such things are stored.

The exciting game goes on for an hour or two
or even longer
sometimes continued over a few evenings
late into the night
players taking turns
reciting a line from a favourite poem.

In one evening
numerous lines of poetry
touching on endless themes of
wisdom and beauty
love and life
joy and pain
would be recited
all from memory.
Not remembering a poem starting with the required letter
means you would lose and
would be out of the game.

In a few years
having learnt enough lines of poetry by heart
my sister and I earned a place around this table
where poets of all times were present for us
in their poems
giving us timeless wisdom in beautiful forms
which we would take away with us into our lives
puzzling over the meanings
marvelling at the language.
We would be praised for the lines we contributed
even if they were simple ones from our school books.
In time we learnt to read and recite
from memory
lines from the poetry of Ferdowsi
Hafez and Sa'di.
Even though real comprehension of the complex meanings
came much later
we were fascinated
by the rhythm and the music of the language
and were encouraged to read and learn the lines by heart.

The exhilaration
of being part of something so magical
has remained with me to this day.
The lines of poetry I could recite
so readily in my teenage and university years
have now become elusive
and most of the time I need to consult the poetry books
which have travelled with me across the world.
Those evenings were
my very first experiences
with the rich and beautiful language
of the classical Persian poets.
Those evenings of *moshaereh*
ignited in me the joy of poetry.

The passion
for classical and contemporary Persian poetry
has stayed with me
ever since.
Poetry is an uplifting source of inspiration in my paintings
and all my creative work.

Joy

Watercolour, acrylic ink
75 x 32 cm
2004
Private collection

Knotted gardens

■ Here is a bird
red and blue
with blue and beige stripes on its back.
The beak is black.
The feet are black.
There are three more on the other three corners
all of them living inside little square homes.
Here is a tree with geometric branches also in a square box.
Can you find the matching one?
How many trees can you find?
And what is this?
Is it a person with a hat?
There are four of them also.
Is it a man or a woman?

We grew up on these fascinating knotted gardens.
Full of wonder the colourful world drew me in
challenged me to make sense of the shapes and colours
kept me engaged and occupied endlessly.
The carpet was a work of art under our feet
a backdrop for our childhood games
introducing us to sophisticated complex visual worlds.

The geometry
the repetitions of lines
squares and triangles
rhythmic lucid patterns
vibrant living colours and flowing forms
a museum piece
a complicated work of art
not on a wall but spread on the floor.
Sometimes depicting a garden

abstract floral patterns
trees and water elements.
Sometimes animals of the forest
lions and foxes
deer and ducks
birds with colourful plumage
flowers and foliage.

With an early memory
I am taken back
to a room of long ago somewhere
a shaft of sunlight pouring in
illuminating a section of the carpet
leaving the rest in shade.
I stretch out
in the warm and sunny solitude of that moment
noticing perhaps for the first time
the complicated geometry of the carpet
its jewel-like colours
the animal forms and foliage.
On the carpet we read books
played quiet games and more physically active games
hopscotch and jumping from one square to the other.
If we were lucky we could even find
in a backroom in a relative's house in Isfahan
a small vertical carpet-weaving loom with a half-finished carpet.
We watched in absolute awe and amazement
the complicated process
the slow progress of the weaving
and the gradual line-by-line
emergence of a figure or a design
over several days of repeated visits to the workshop.

The carpet
the artistic sensibility
the craftsmanship humbles me
grounds me
places me within the context of my ancestral artistic heritage.
Who designed this?
Where did the wool come from?
Which flowering plants provided the dyes for colouring the wool?
In which small village workshop was the loom set up?
Which small fingers worked the countless hours
to create this masterpiece?
Who bought it first from the one who created it?
Was he or she paid well and what was bought in exchange
for this exquisite colourful work of art that so intrigues me?
How can I walk over it without acknowledging all of this?
So it is that every time I see a carpet
anywhere
it is a private cherished moment for me
an aesthetic experience
a moment of gratitude and a moment of humility.

I review in my mind my work of the past thirty years
on this other side of the planet
far away from the people and the workshops
that created these works of art.

Elements and motifs from the carpets
have found their place
in many of my paintings and works in precious metals
as abstracted foliage
flowers and trees
as butterflies and birds.

The timeless flowing design elements
have found a new life in my work
depicting ideas of freedom and spontaneity
geometric patterns representing notions
of limits and boundaries.

The abstracted arabesque has emerged
as the heads of snakes etched on glass boards
or pierced on gold and silver elements
for a *Snakes and Ladders* game.
The arabesque has found its way
to the top of a glass and metal table
or sometimes pierced on a silver pendant.
The versatility and the potential
for abstraction and modernization
of these timeless motifs are truly limitless.

In the silence and solitude of the studio
every time I am engaged in working
with these gifts from the past
my heart fills with gratitude.
I become aware of my connection
beyond the boundaries of time and place
to the man or woman
from many generations ago
who for the first time
looked at the sinuous form of a flower or a plant
and inspired by that natural form
developed and created the arabesque
and brought it to life
in a new form
within the borders of a knotted garden.

On a silver tray

■ From a trip back to Isfahan
mother had brought a circular silver tray
the radius almost twenty-five centimeters.

Preoccupied with my life
and uninterested
at the time of the purchase of the tray
I did not pay attention to the history
or the beginnings of the creation
and acquisition of the tray.

Now it sits on a table in front of me.

Our loving mother has left us.
Her tray lives on.
It will outlive me
will continue its existence
and one day
perhaps it will sit on a table in front of
our great-grandchildren.

It will continue
its silent and serene existence
into a future inconceivable for me
and for the craftsmen
who created
this exquisite world
on a silver tray.

I now know
that the two highly respected craftsmen
who created the tray

and chiselled the intricate designs
lived and worked in Isfahan.
Both distant relatives of our father
and masters of their craft
they devoted their lives
to the perfection of their creations.
One day at the age of seventy-five
working in his shop
the master abruptly fell down
and never got up again.
His creations continue to live on.
His name stamped on the back of the tray
is hardly legible to the naked eye.

My imagination takes me to a future
when perhaps mother's silver tray
will be a focus of wonder and awe
like a piece in a museum
that started its life in the hands of a craftsman
a thousand years before
and now sits in a glass case
labelled and numbered
to be viewed by spectators who would not know or share
any of the life experiences of the creators
of these artefacts.

As I write these words
I question their truth.
Perhaps despite the inevitable transformations
in the way ordinary human life continues on earth
some things will remain unchanged.

What are the timeless
values and sensibilities and dreams that
inspired and motivated
the master craftsman who created this piece?
Will these sentiments endure and continue
into the unpredictable ever changing future?

Under the powerful lamp in my studio
with a jeweller's magnifying visor on my head
my father's magnifying glass
in my hand
I enter the world portrayed on the silver tray.

It is fascinating
the elaborate designs
the details of the images
the precision of the lines
everything chiselled and hammered
yet appearing as if drawn with the point of a sharp fine pen.

In the centre there is a circle
depicting designs reminiscent of
the interior of a dome
the slightly raised geometric elements in
satin white silver
in *bas-relief* on the blackened background.

Arabesques and abstracted foliage and flowers
fill the surface of a wide ring
sharing the same centre point with the central circle.

Situated in the wide inner border of the tray

ten relatively large windows draw me in.
I see parakeets or parrots
birds with trailing long tails
and names unknown to me
perched on top of the window frames
one on each upper side
a total of twenty birds.

Five of these windows depict
almost identical abstracted
trees flowers and foliage
four extraordinary birds
with perfectly chiselled plumage perched on the trees.
Residing inside these five windows
I see another twenty birds.
But it is the other five windows
that attract me the most.
Each window illustrates
a scene with flowers and foliage
men and women or animals
lions and horses
a donkey and a sheep.

One of the five windows depicts a scene from
Khosrow and Shirin
the famous intriguing and sad love story by
Nezami Ganjavi.
The Sasanian king Khosrow
having fallen in love with
Shirin the Armenian princess
after seeing her picture
is on his way to Armenia to find her.

After only a glance at his picture
Shirin is also in love with Khosrow
and is on her way to find her beloved.
The window on the tray
paints the famous moment
when Shirin
tired from the long journey
is bathing in a lake
surrounded by her companions
and Khosrow arrives at the scene on his horse.
As I remember the tale has a sad ending
the lovers will go their opposite ways
and will face unbelievable challenges.

Another window portrays a
rider on a horse with a bow and arrow
fighting two lions.

A mystic is depicted on the third window
with his *tabarzin* and *kashkul*
seated silently beside a learned man reading a book.

A shepherd and his sheep fill another window.

And in the last one
an ordinary man
rides his donkey in solitude.

I am mesmerized with all the images I see
through these modern aids for magnification
chiselled so exquisitely on the silver tray.
Perhaps similar magnifying tools were used

by the master creator of this work.
In awe and wonder
I follow the movement
of the fine-pointed chisel
carving the minuscule curved lines in the hard silver
the strands of hair
the features of a face
the feathers on a bird
the mane of a lion.
The quality and precision of the work
is superhuman and fills me
with admiration and with absolute humility.
I contemplate the work
the quality and the beauty of the symbols.

In the design and crafting of the piece
I can sense the master craftsmen's
respect for order and precision
the total dedication to the creation of beauty.

Love
patience
vision and courage
spiritual search
all come to mind as I contemplate the meanings
of the symbols portrayed
within the ornate borders of the five windows.
Are these dreams
these quests and values
passion and dedication not timeless?
Will they not endure into the unknown future?

For me the answers to these questions are positive.
Yet I know that the piece still has more to tell me
and that my perception of the symbolic meanings
is still limited and not complete.

I also know that I will continue to cherish
my mother's silver tray.
I will enjoy the world and the qualities it represents
filled with respect for the master craftsmen who created it
and grateful that mother had the insight to see
the beauty and the meanings it portrayed.

I will cherish it and pass it along as a symbol
of the timeless
the beautiful and the intangible.

Yellow Butterfly - detail

Watercolour, acrylic ink
75 x 32 cm
2004
Private collection

The wise teacher

■ Confused and guilt-ridden
for being alive
broken and lost
I carried out
only basic everyday chores of living
struggling to understand and to cope
with the new tragic reality.

Life had lost all its meaning.
Everything seemed superficial.
How could a young life end so abruptly in that river
in that magnificent landscape
on an island a few hours away?

The beauty of nature had vanished for me
all of nature had become cruel and unpredictable.

In the solitude
of the forest near our house
screaming and crying
I pleaded for answers
sat in silence in his room and meditated
read books and wrote to keep my sanity
searched for a meaning and a purpose
how to live again
how to find the strength to get back to life
to care for my family
suffering this loss with me
to do something
that may matter
in this continuous never-ending dark night
that had become my life.

Art making had become meaningless and unnecessary
and I had abandoned my studio.
Restless and angry I walked every day
unaware of my surroundings
alone in the exuberant nature
on the edge of our neighbourhood in Vancouver
oblivious to everything around me
lost in my own world of grief.

But in a rare moment on a walk
I was somehow drawn
into the mystery of a different existence
sensing the world belonging to the elements of nature
in my path and in front of my eyes.
In an instant it seemed
the weeping willow
with its branches and leaves
arching down to the earth
became me and I became it
as if we shared the same understanding
the same sadness.
I became the yellow dandelion
growing out of the gravel on my path.

I became the small dog on a leash
with the muddy white coat
walking ahead of me with its owner
on that cold windy Vancouver day.
I felt its feelings
its innocence and surrender
to the pace of its owner
and to the wet and rainy day.

I always had an intimate connection with nature.
My best memories were from days spent
in the gardens of my childhood
elements of nature always present in my paintings
the sky and the sun
the water and the trees
mountains and gardens.

Everything had changed with the agony of this grief.

Once again in moments during my walks
it felt as if I was conversing and connecting
with the elements and phenomena of nature
not through words of a language
but through this deep and vast silence that engulfed everything.
I was drawn out of the cage of my own concerns
and dispersed and dissolved into the vast and boundless space.
The light and the colours around me were different.
It was as if I was seeing everything for the first time.
For a moment there was no sadness
no joy and no need
just a different understanding and connection
a different mode of existence.

Strangely peaceful and bewildered at the same time
I did not feel alone anymore
but part of this magnificent world
with a feeling of acceptance
sensing and sharing the experience of all the mothers
who have lost a child
everyone who has suffered
everyone who has experienced sorrow.

I felt a deep appreciation for all the love
that permeated my life
the unconditional compassion and care
given to me by my grieving aging parents
the love and support my husband had for me
sharing with me the unbearable sorrow and despair.
I felt the pain of our younger son
his confusion and vulnerability and his love.
I felt grateful for my sister and her daughters
who shared and carried the pain of our small family
and held us in their love.

My extended family and friends
and even complete strangers
had given us much compassion
and I had been blind to all this
wrapped up in my anger and despair
in the dark corner of my grief.

This whole landscape of love and life
opened up for me
as if nature was telling me
that I was supported and will get through this.

For several months I had avoided the ocean
had avoided the beach.
To continue to live in this city
on this endless shore is too painful and unbearable.

Somewhere in my unconscious mind
I must have known there was no choice but to make peace
with this water despite the terror it evoked in me.

After many months
on a calm and cloudy Vancouver day
half-heartedly and in desperation
I found my way to the beach near our home.
The log I chose to sit on was just at the edge of the water.
Sitting still
surrendered to the sadness
with eyes closed
I noticed the rhythm of my breathing
becoming one
with the rhythm and the sound of the waves.
It felt as if the waves of water
entered my whole body
and left again
in rhythms beyond my control.
Then there was no me and no body
just the rhythm and the music of the waves
as if I had been a part of this ebb and flow from eternity.
There was no pain
nothing
just the waves
for how long
I do not know.

Still breathing in the waves
I opened my eyes
the blue-grey ocean in front of me
the North Shore mountains beyond
an immense
magnificent landscape
and I and my pain
so small and insignificant.

All of this had been here for thousands and thousands of years
millions of years
and my life just an instant
a speck
on these waves of existence.
What arrogance to feel this rage
towards something so vast and so ancient!
What did I have to say?
What could I say?

Surrendering to the ebb and flow of life
realizing the limits
and the choices within those limits
and living this short life with acceptance and love
is my only choice.

This all made sense to me
as I got up and walked away from the log and the ocean
of which I had become a part for a brief eternity
in that timeless expanse.

I had again found the wise teacher
in the nature around me.

Contemplation in the garden

On a hot summer day in Tehran
I am sitting not in a garden
but inside an apartment
in front of a deeply recessed window
opening to a small balcony
and a long and narrow courtyard beyond
planted with trees and shrubs.

All I see from this window
are three slender birch trees and two old pines
with green and brown cones
green and brown needles
their tall trunks hunched and twisted.
The small branches and the leaves of the birch trees
sway and dance with the slightest breeze.
A white butterfly appears in the frame of my window
disappears
appears and disappears again.
Just behind the trees is a wall
and some distance away from the first
is another wall
the colour of light amber.
The high wall obscures Mount Damavand from my view.
I know because I could see the magnificent mountain
from this window
before the tall building
that conceals the snow covered peak
was built some years ago.
The amber-coloured wall meets a strip of blue-grey sky
just visible in the frame
beyond the lattice of leaves and branches
that rise up high and out of my view.

My experience of this moment
is completed by a symphony of sounds.
I hear the constant noise of Tehran traffic in the background
and in the foreground
hear the occasional sweet song of a bird I cannot see
and the cry of a crow.

This window
the five trees
the memory of the mountain blocked by the wall
the white butterfly
the strip of blue-grey sky
the noise of Tehran traffic
the occasional song of the bird I cannot see
and the cry of the crow
describe my 'garden'
my experience of this moment
as I write my 'Contemplation in the garden'
the final piece of writing in this book
my gift for our grandchildren.

My mind at this moment is also very preoccupied
with thoughts about ongoing negotiations
between Iran and the superpowers of the world.
I am grateful that such negotiations are taking place
in our increasingly confusing and intolerant world
and am hoping for a wise and just reconciliation.

Maybe this time
goals can be achieved
not with wars but with words.

My view from this window
although limited and confined
still allows me entry to the garden
that lives in my memory
and in my imagination
the garden that has taught me so much
about life and how to live it.

Life in the garden is ephemeral
change is the only constant.

There are sweet and warm days
and moments full of green and red and yellow
joyful colours of the limitless rainbow.
There are cold and dark days
that bring with them the grey heaviness
and mournful melancholy of a thousand years.

They both pass.

I have learnt
to search for
appreciate and celebrate
vitality and colour
beauty and joy
even when it is limited and framed
or seemingly hidden behind a wall
a wall that can be of brick and mortar
hiding the beauty of the magnificent mountain
or a wall of anger and resentment
hiding a warm and loving heart
that I need to discover.

I learnt in the hardest way
the truth of the grey and cold days
the inevitable pain and suffering
that is part of being human
each of us having a share
a smaller or bigger share
and sometimes the biggest share.

Storm and snow
thunder and drought
accidents
malaise and illness
can and do happen in a garden and in life.
Such events are sometimes unpreventable
and perhaps unavoidable.
But there is another kind of suffering that happens in life
because of actions that are not unavoidable
actions that I take
actions that we all take
actions that bring pain and suffering upon
someone
somewhere.

Not to cause pain
to avoid bringing more harm and suffering
into the world
to strive for understanding and harmony
seems to be the only necessary rule.
The continuation and quality of our lives
in our shared garden on this planet
depends on how committed each of us is to this one rule
not to cause or bring more harm and suffering into the world.

I learn in the garden
how each plant
each tree and each flower
each bird and bee and butterfly
play their parts
in the magnificent play
that is the play of life in the garden.
Their parts are all different.
They work together to produce flowers and fruits
colour and scent
shade and shelter.
But they all share and benefit from
the same warm sunshine
the same earth and water
the same cool nights
the same moon and stars.

The pine is still the pine
the pomegranate tree bears its red fruit
the white jasmine radiates its sweet fragrance
and the mint and basil thrive and spread over the earth.
They all benefit equally from the sunshine
the earth and water
their right from the beginning of time.

Would it ever be possible for us
human beings
on this earth
to benefit from the same resources and opportunities
that our garden offers?
Would it be possible to truly play our parts
to realize our potential?

Can such a world
seemingly so out of reach and unreal
at this time
in the second decade
of the twenty-first century
ever exist?

As my imagination
takes me beyond the view
of the pine trees
and the birch trees
framed by the window in front of me
I ask and wonder
what such a world would look like
how we each would feel
and how we each would live
in this world
wayfarers passing through the garden
for a brief moment
playing our parts
leaving our marks?

PART TWO

Paintings
Art in Precious Metals

I paint my dreams of a wonderful childhood my children will never experience... a childhood spent in brick walled gardens of apple blossom trees, turquoise blue ponds and heavy wooden doors.

I also paint another dream, which never came true... the dream of creating urban spaces that could stand proudly next to creations of a thousand years before. We were near, but it all suddenly came to an end. Not only our 'town', but our sources of inspiration, works of generations of unknown master builders and artisans, belonging not to one nation, but to the whole human race.

And so, thousands of miles away, I paint my dreams of places that are no more, and a dream that never came true.

Artist Statement

ARTROPOLIS
Vancouver, 1987

Painting on the shores of the Pacific Ocean
with the *Ruba'iyat* of Omar Khayyam

■ We finally left.
We finally left the chaos
the uncertainties
the hypocrisy.
We finally left
in the middle of a pointless war
too afraid to stay
too afraid to protest
against the war or
against anything else.

We finally left
guilt-ridden for having left
dispirited about unfinished dreams and unfinished projects
apprehensive and concerned about the unknown future
feeling helpless in the face of uncertainties of settling in a new place.

Why did we all leave?
Was it the right decision?
What can we do here
in this beautiful but distant city
that has suddenly become our city
in this land that we know so little about
and that we must learn to love
to live in
to call home?

What is the purpose of life...the purpose of my life?

We had left
travelled to this other side of the globe
made a choice to make this our home.

Yet the culture I had left behind
the experiences and the memories are with me
strong and alive
connecting me to the home
on the other side of the planet.
I do not want to break these ties.
There is so much that is still positive
beautiful and enriching
despite all that is unbearable
that is intolerable
that impelled us to leave.

But what about this new chosen country
this new chosen city?
Before long
this will be the only place
our children will call home.
This choice demands of me
to live a positive
meaningful life here
become involved
become a member of this community
contribute to its well-being and feel a sense of belonging.

But can I live in two worlds?

Elusive questions
and answers difficult to reach
issues of every day survival and experience crowd my mind
mingle with the bigger questions
the philosophical puzzle
that is our life and our existence.

Like so many times before
I reach for the poetry of Omar Khayyam
reading his words in Persian
in my mother-tongue
in an old well-used and well-loved volume
a small book with a ragged dark-green hardcover
that belonged to my father
a book that has travelled with me across the world.

Like so many times before
Khayyam speaks to me.
His wisdom is inspiring
focuses my mind
gives me clarity
tranquility.

The year was 1984
when we came as
new-comers to Vancouver.

Now as I write three decades later and wish to share
my experience with the inspiring *Ruba'iyat*
in those unsettled days
I quote from the English translations
by Peter Avery and John Heath Stubbs
which seem to closely convey
the spirit of Khayyam's poetry.

> This ocean of being has come from the Obscure
> No one has pierced this jewel of reality
> Each has spoken according to his humour
> No one can define the face of things.

Those who dominated the circle of learning and culture
In the company of the perfect became lamps among their peers
By daylight they could not escape from darkness
So they told a fable and went to sleep.

Neither you nor I know the mysteries of eternity
Neither you nor I read this enigma
You and I only talk this side of the veil
When the veil falls, neither you nor I will be here.

The cycle which includes our coming and going
Has no discernible beginning nor end
Nobody has got this matter straight
Where we come from and where we go to.

In these insightful lines
Khayyam gives no answers
to the larger questions
but the ephemeral nature of life
its impermanence
unpredictability
and its indifference are indisputable for him.

Take it, heart, that all the world's trappings are won
That your pleasure-garden is decked out in green
Then, seated one night like a dew on that greenness
Take it that dawn has already risen.

Come friend let us lose tomorrow's grief
And seize this moment of life
Tomorrow, this ancient inn abandoned
We shall be equal with those born seven thousand years ago!

What have you to do with Being, friend
And empty opinions about the notion of mind and spirit?
Joyfully live and let the world pass happily
The beginning of the matter was not arranged with you in mind.

With his insights into the impermanence of this ephemeral existence
Khayyam encourages me to appreciate
the joy and beauty of nature
of friendship
wine and music.
In the face of the transience of all there is
he tells me to focus on the beauty of what there is
before it is gone.

When the drunken nightingale found his way into the garden
He discovered the face of the rose and the wine-cup laughing
He came to whisper in my ear excitedly
'Seek out these, life once gone cannot be sought again.'

The days of time disdain him
Who sits sorrowing over the grief of time
Drink a glass of wine to the notes of the harp
Before all glasses are smashed on rock.

In the end he tells me to cherish each moment
and despite the unpredictable nature of life
to live it responsibly.

Don't seek to recall yesterday that is past
Nor repine for tomorrow, which has not yet come
Don't build your hopes on the past or the future
Be happy now and don't live on wind.

The good and evil that are in man's heart
The joy and sorrow that are our fortune and destiny
Do not impute them to the wheel of heaven because
in the light of reason
The wheel is a thousand times more helpless than you.

It is we who are the source of our own happiness the mine
of our own sorrow
The repository of justice and foundation of iniquity
We who are cast down and exalted, perfect and defective
At once the rusted mirror and Jamshid's all-seeing cup.

As I read this poetry thousands of miles away
from my home of a thousand years before
my memories and experiences in nature
in the gardens left behind
in the gardens of the Persian miniatures
emerge and merge with the imagery of
the gardens of Khayyam's poetry
and the gardens of this green city
my new city
our new home
on the shores of this blue-green ocean.

Khayyam encourages me to see
that the experience of beauty and exuberance of nature
is not left behind.
Beauty is here before my eyes
in this city
in this new home
on the shores of the Pacific ocean
surrounded by nature.

The *Ruba'iyat* inspire and encourage me
to express in my own language
the feelings and memories they have invoked in me
to safeguard and preserve this experience
somewhere deep within me
to make it my own.

I begin to paint.

The geometry
motifs and colours
the turquoise-blue pool
the ochre earth
the red pomegranate trees
the arabesque design on a carpet
all become the words of a language
the words of my language.
A language with which I strive to express
the timeless
placeless wisdom and beauty
of these poems
and to keep alive the memories
of the place left behind.

I experience the healing power of poetry and art
the healing power of this creative journey
that is now the bridge
connecting my two worlds.

Once we were well-settled in Vancouver, I painted about one hundred and twenty small detailed watercolour and gold leaf paintings, over a twelve-year period, mostly based on the poetry of Omar Khayyam. The paintings, some of which are included in the following pages, were exhibited in Canada and United States. The excerpts of the poems quoted are from the English translations of the *Ruba'iyat* by Peter Avery and John Heath Stubbs.

When the intoxicated
nightingale found
the garden

Birds and Pomegranate Trees

Watercolour, gouache, 24k gold
49.5 x 20 cm
1991
Artist's collection

Since the wheel does
not turn to the will
of the wise

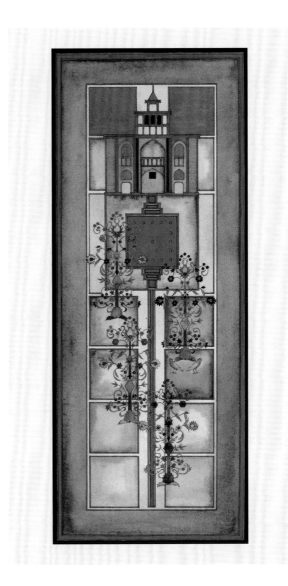

Garden of Fin

Watercolour, 24k gold leaf
48 x 19 cm
1989
Private collection

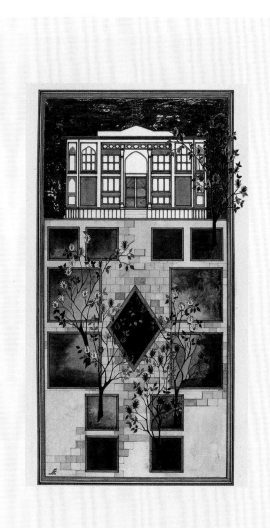

The meadow is like
paradise talk less
of heaven

Hasht Behesht

Watercolour, 24k gold leaf
35 x 20 cm
1991
Private collection

Such precious jewels
are hidden
in your chest

The Purple Garden

Watercolour, gouache, 24k gold
32 x 20 cm
1989
Artist's collection

This old tavern
whose name
is the world

Horses in the Garden

Watercolour, 24k gold
47.5 x 26.5 cm
1990
Artist's collection

You will not resolve
the mystery
of the riddle

Garden of Pomegranate Trees and Horse

Watercolour, 24k gold
50 x 22.5 cm
1990
Private collection

If the heart
could grasp the
meaning of life

Pomegranate Trees - detail

Watercolour, 24k gold
53 x 18.5 cm
1990
Private Collection

Who is the one
who returned to tell
us the secret

The Garden Gate

Watercolour, 24k gold
53 x 23 cm
1989
Artist's collection

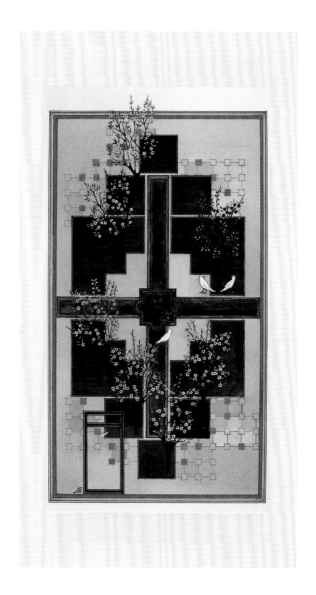

If the lover and
the intoxicated reside
in hell then no one
will see paradise

Chahar Bagh and Birds

Watercolour, 24k gold
34 x 19 cm
1988
Private collection

This green
our pleasure
garden today

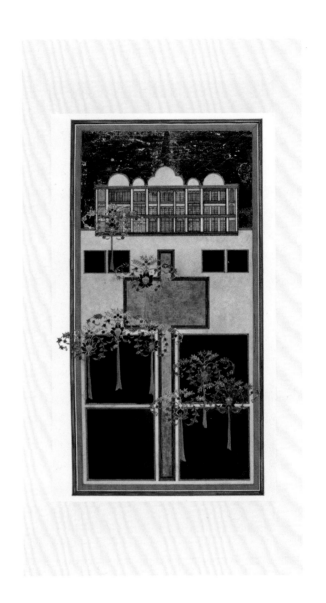

Garden of Eram

Watercolour, 24k gold leaf
35.5 x 20.5 cm
1998
Private collection

Tomorrow, when
we leave this
ancient inn

Seize this Moment

Watercolour, 24k gold
33.5 x 18 cm
1988
Private collection

Rise and do not
grieve this transient
world

Memories

Watercolour, 24k gold
34 x 18 cm
1988
Artist's collection

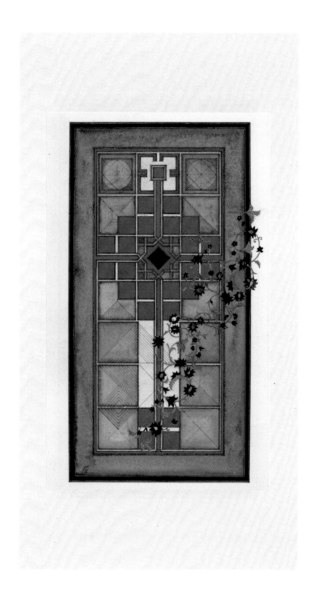

Sing the song
and bring out
the wine

Lingering Echo

Watercolour, 24k gold
30 x 17 cm
1989
Private collection

How long shall I lay
bricks on the face
of the seas

Apple Blossoms

Watercolour, 24k gold
29 x 17 cm
1988
Private collection

The house of sorrow
will one day become
a rose garden

A Rose Shall Bloom

Watercolour, 24k gold
46.5 x 20 cm
1990
Private collection

Sit in the shade
of a rose
since...

In the Shade of a Rose

Watercolour, gouache, 24k gold
46.5 x 26.5 cm
1989
Private collection

No one knows
the truth
as it is

Garden of Four Seasons

Watercolour, 24k gold
36 x 21 cm
1989
Private collection

Who went to hell and
who came back
from heaven

Freedom

Watercolour, 24k gold leaf
36 x 24 cm
1989
Artist's collection

You asked what
is this transient
pattern

There is Hope Beyond

Watercolour, 24k gold leaf
40.5 x 30.5 cm
1991
Artist's collection

It is a pattern
that came out
of an ocean

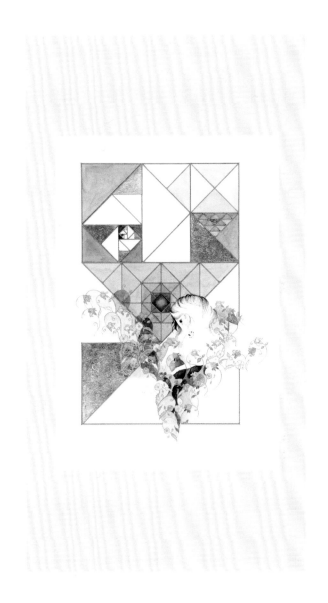

Eternity

Watercolour, 24k gold leaf
62 x 44 cm
1994
Artist's collection

And now in a field
full of iris they are
still searching

In Search of an Iris

Watercolour, 24k gold
55 x 33 cm
1992
Artist's collection

For a time we acted
on this stage
we went back
one by one
into the box
of oblivion

Two Horses - detail

Watercolour, 24k gold
34 x 26 cm
1988
Private collection

They sang
a serenade
and went
to sleep

The Song

Watercolour, 24k gold
49 x 22 cm
1992
Private collection

They went and
we shall go
others shall
come and
shall go

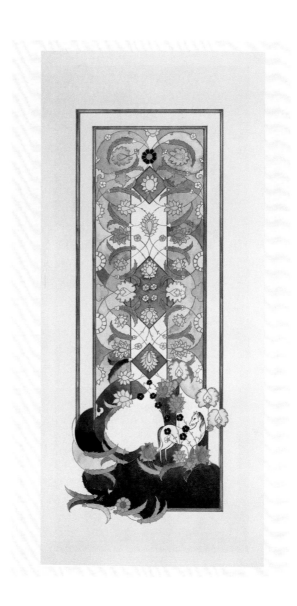

Finding the Lake

Watercolour, 24k gold
56 x 22 cm
1992
Private collection

Each brick on
the pinnacle
of a parapet

Garden of Fin Revisited

Watercolour, 24k gold
51.5 x 21 cm
1990
Artist's collection

This green is our
pleasure garden
today

Carpet and Garden

Watercolour, gouache, 24k gold
49.5 x 18.5 cm
1991
Artist's collection

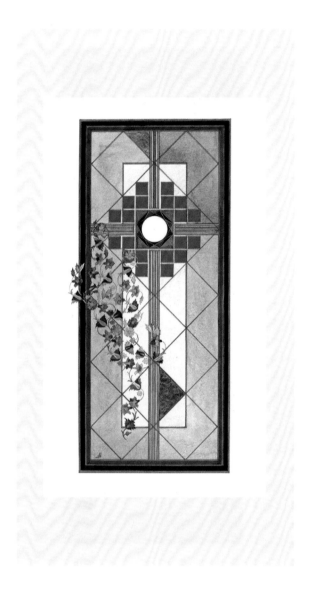

Scatter roses
on the footsteps
of dawn

Song of Flowers

Watercolour, gouache, 24k gold leaf
44.5 x 21 cm
1990
Artist's collection

You will slip into
the mysterious
veil of inexistence

The Peacock and the Garden

Watercolour, 24k gold
41 x 28 cm
1991
Private collection

Every particle of dust
on a patch of earth
was a sun-cheek
or brow of
the morning star

Metamorphosis

Watercolour, 24k gold
81.5 x 55 cm
1992
Artist's collection

Let us consider this wheel
of heaven that amazes us
as if it were a diorama

Garden of Oranges

Watercolour
97 x 60 cm
2003
Private collection

Painting the gardens of cypress and song
with the poetry of Shafii Kadkani

Rushing rivers and streams
birds in flight and in song
or in a cage
trees in bloom
or sometimes leafless
on rocky mountain faces and fields
sunflowers turning towards the sun
almond blossoms and pomegranate gardens
mirrors and mountains
multi-layered paintings in words
depicting seasons of rain and snow
sunshine and spring.

All the elements of nature
are the focus of attention
and all are in conversation with the poet.

The conversations become poems
the reflections of Shafii Kadkani
on life
on being human
on becoming human.

The language is beautiful
in the Persian words of the poet.
In my translations
I aspire to be as loyal to the original as I can.

In the poems
elements and phenomena of nature
are seen as accessible and universal
manifestations of the spiritual realm.

Is there anyone here who would say
I see the spirit of existence in the lilies' brightness
and in the sacred song of the chrysanthemum
more so than in the mosque or monastery?

The poems talk about love and life
the one life given to each
and about how it could be lived
with awareness
with compassion
with kindness and responsibility.

Love is not word. It is meaning
a ladder to the upper world.

Is love the art of dying
so magical and beautiful?
Love is the losing of me, you, him, her
whatever you have lost, it is all there.

The poems ruminate on the meaning of
freedom
the appreciation of freedom
the need for patience and perseverance
in obtaining freedom
never losing hope that one day
it may be attainable.

Just as the cloud is wrapped up in its weeping
just as the rose is rapt lifelong by joy
just as the being of fire is burning's prisoner
for man, all he is searching for is freedom.

The poems are about art and art making
that mysterious human endeavour that defies simple definitions
does not guarantee worldly gains
but bestows upon the creative spirit
the most uplifting and exhilarating experience
when it flows freely with life
and the darkest desperate state
when it is blocked and dead.

The freer your pathway to art may be
the closer it is to the spiritual search.
When you peer through that miraculous window
just then, even God is more godly.

The poems contemplate death
the unknown mysterious
inevitable destiny of all.
Questions are posed.
The reflections enlighten and inspire
show us our shared vulnerabilities
show us our lack of choice
in the most inevitable part of life
our inescapable final state
of surrender to the unknown.

When I die, O Hidden One, transform me into rain
in your path, make me one of the seekers.

The earth, wind, fire and water
from which you fashioned me
do not take them away from me
release me into timeless universe.

The water, even as a drop in noontide
pour me as rain on a shrub in the desert.

The handful of my earth, bestow it at the feet of the poppy
form me, thus, as the eye and the light of spring.

The wind, join it with the turbulent thunder to uproot
injustice and oppression from the earth
and once again make me one of the restless.

From my fire strike a spark of love and compassion
in the heart of lovers
make me thus the comfort and consolation
of my vast circle of friends.

I do not favour sleeping in silence beneath a stone
do whatever you desire
but make me one of the seekers.

The poems of Shafii Kadkani
contemplate all these infinite questions
and much more.
The language is lucid and inspiring.
It is as if he is sitting next to me
talking about all that matters in life
like a good friend
a wise teacher.
The beauty of the language
the strength of the images
and a shared connection with nature
inspire and convince me
to begin to translate and paint the poems.

As I translate the poems into English
and immerse myself
in the environment and ambiance of the poems
I can read and sense beyond the beauty
of the words and the images
powerful and thought-provoking
layers of hidden meanings.
I aspire to express my perceptions
of these poems and their meanings
in the visual language of my art.

Gradually and over many years
a language has developed.
Geometry and sinuous fluid lines
abstracted forms inspired by nature
transparent layers of shapes
colours and textures
and simplified motifs
from the repertoire of Persian visual art
have become the words of a language
with endless possibilities of expression.
Yet the most important component of the process
remains elusive and hard to put into words.

In the solitude of my studio
I am aware of a structure and form
that wants to be expressed
that needs to be conveyed
and that I obey and draw on the white board.
At some point in the process
when I am completely absorbed in the work
the painting itself seems to take over.

As I connect with the poem
and the deep feelings and thoughts it invokes
the image develops further
despite and beyond my conscious decisions.
Colours and textures are chosen
happen and take shape
in a process in which I am a participant.
There is a moment
when the painting tells me it is finished
and I listen.

Painting the poetry of Shafii Kadkani has been a process of joy and learning. Through English translation of his poems and creation of paintings inspired by them, I have attempted to express and convey my appreciation of this body of work to audiences both in Iran and beyond. The paintings, some of which are presented here, were exhibited in three solo shows in Tehran and two solo exhibitions in Vancouver. A selection of paintings, poems and translations were published in 2008, in Tehran, as an illustrated bilingual book entitled *In the Mirror of the Stream*.

And what is poetry, what is it, if not
that moment of polishing the dust away
from the mirror of certainty and convictions
seeing
at the moment of the blooming of a rose
the freedom of the whole earth?

Excerpt from *Poetry*
Shair, Shafii Kadkani

Poetry

Watercolour
103 x 75 cm
2004
Artist's collection

Like a magician who
makes doves fly,
        from the inside of an empty hat...

Excerpt from *The Magician*
Shobadehbaz, Shafii Kadkani

The Magician

Watercolour, acrylic ink
74 x 32 cm
2004
Artist's collection

What is this sea inside a droplet?
What is this sun inside a speck?

Excerpt from *The Living Fire*
Atash-e zendeh, Shafii Kadkani

The Living Fire

Watercolour
105 x 68 cm
2004
Private collection

At the time of flight
from one garden to another
no one searched under the wings of
the swallows
and butterflies.

Excerpt from *Nowhere*
Nakoja, Shafii Kadkani

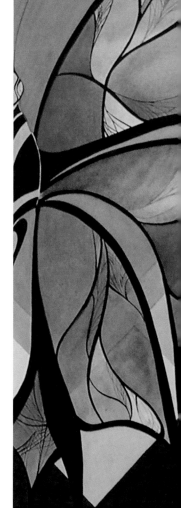

Nowhere

Watercolour, acrylic ink
70 x 100 cm
2004
Artist's collection

In the end, I will pass on from here.
A butterfly, who was passing in the night
read this fortune for my heart.

Excerpt from *Intention to Depart*
Qasd-e rahil, Shafii Kadkani

Intention to Depart

Watercolour, acrylic ink
75 x 33 cm
2004
Artist's collection

My whole being yearns, but
what can I do with my feet tied?

Excerpt from *A Good Journey I Wish You*
Safar be kheyre, Shafii Kadkani

A Good Journey I Wish You

Watercolour, acrylic ink
69 x 99 cm
2004
Artist's collection

'Look,'
        I say:
                This is the magic of the lover and the dawn
'The one has hardly left
                and the other begins
the voice is one
                but the birds are many.'

Excerpt from *The Eloquence of the Birds*
Manteq al-tayre, Shafii Kadkani

The Eloquence of the Birds

Watercolour
114 x 66 cm
2004
Private collection

Come up with a tune from a different song
in another key on a different instrument.
My heart is saddened by this melody and wants
another kind of path, another view.

Excerpt from *Another View*
Cheshmandaz-e digar, Shafii Kadkani

Another View

Watercolour
75 x 33 cm
2004
Private collection

And now
tonight, in vain, I wonder
under the snow so full of words
where did they bury
the corpse of the lark's evening songs?

Excerpt from *Story of Exile in the West*
Qessat-al-qorbat-al-qarbiyat
Shafii Kadkani

Story of Exile in the West

Watercolour
54 x 75 cm
2005
Artist's collection

Love is not a word. It is meaning
a ladder to the upper world.

When death takes life in wedlock
Love is apparent in the mirror's depth.

Is love the art of dying
so magical and beautiful?

To die and live again in death
is truly an exalted state.

Excerpt from *Poem in Praise of Love*
Ghasideh dar setayesh-e eshq, Shafii Kadkani

Poem in Praise of Love

Watercolour
72 x 46 cm
1998–2005
Artist's collection

It is beauty that will be
          the salvation of mankind and the earth.

Excerpt from *Salvation*
Rastegari, Shafii Kadkani

Salvation

Watercolour
75 x 47 cm
2006
Private collection

All the words I knew I offered to the tree
but not for an instant did it let me into its depth.

Excerpt from *In the Presence of the Tree*
Dar barabar-e derakht, Shafii Kadkani

In the Presence of the Tree

Watercolour, acrylic ink
74 x 49 cm
2005
Private collection

The butterfly asks the petal of flower:
'When is our time together going to be longer than this?'
From the far side of the pond the frog
                                        replies:
'...perhaps in the closed leaves of a book
in an old abandoned attic room.'

Excerpt from *Of Being Eternal*
Javdanegi, Shafii Kadkani

Of Being Eternal

Watercolour, acrylic ink
73 x 47 cm
2006
Private collection

All the rain's calligraphies of light
are in praise of deliverance
the breadth of the world is brimful of joy and freedom
if only this demon and this wall allowed.

Excerpt from *The Veils*
Pardegian, Shafii Kadkani

The Veils

Watercolour, acrylic ink, marker
73 x 45 cm
2006
Private collection

I would rather be a tree
under the whip of thunder and lightning
in a quest to blossom and speak
than
the tame face of a rock
caressed and embraced by rain
silent and listening.

The Sacred Song of the Tree
Mazmur-e derakht, Shafii Kadkani

The Sacred Song of the Tree

Watercolour, acrylic ink
79 x 30 cm
2006
Private collection

In the twinkling of an eye
I made a ladder out of silence
I climbed the roof of mystery
I saw myself in body
an atom in the galaxy.

Excerpt from *Upon the Shoreless Shore*
Bar karan-e bikaran, Shafii Kadkani

Upon the Shoreless Shore

Watercolour, marker
73 x 47 cm
2006
Artist's collection

When you peer through that miraculous window
just then, even the Divine, is more Divine.

Excerpt from *Through that Miraculous Window*
Zaan panjereh-e shegerf, Shafii Kadkani

Through that Miraculous Window

Watercolour, marker
71 x 40 cm
2006
Artist's collection

After all the buzzing and humming
and the light and song
and all the performers of this garden's pavilions
beneath this cloudless blue, if there is any sound
it is the lament of the garden weeping and
                                  the clamour of the crows.

Excerpt from *The Garden of the Crows*
Bagh-e zaghan, Shafii Kadkani

The Garden of the Crows

Watercolour, acrylic ink
75 x 29 cm
2006
Artist's collection

Perhaps it is singing for joy
or perhaps it is joyous from singing.

Excerpt from *The Song of the Bird*
Avaz-e parandeh, Shafii Kadkani

The Song of the Bird

Watercolour, acrylic ink
78 x 54 cm
2007
Private collection

All the path was filled with freedom.
That moment was the last.

The morning of the convergence of earth
and clustering and light
the mercurial morning of Nishapur

became the thicket of thorns and sticks
the landscape of the vulture's wingspan

and then, this vermillion setting of the sun
and this monstrous night of snow.

Excerpt from *Blue-Black Song*
Taraneh kaboud, Shafii Kadkani

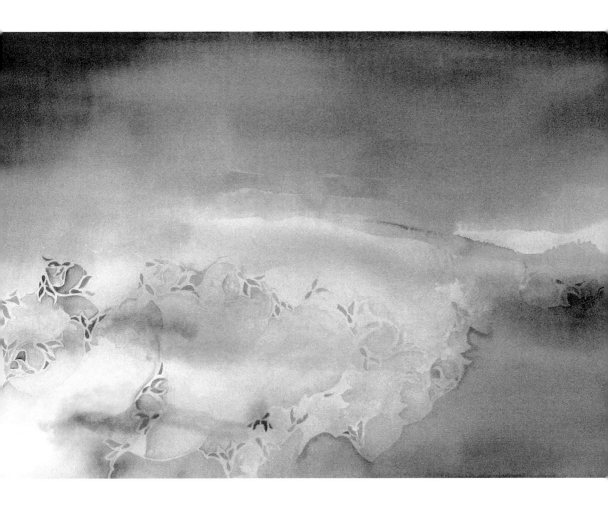

Blue-Black Song

Watercolour
40 x 84 cm
2007
Private collection

Throughout the winter, the sparrow
                    looked forward with yearning
to spring and the garden so much
                    that in mid-winter
it saw the flowers painted on the mosque tile
as the dawn of spring.

Floral Patterns on a Tile
Golhay-e naqsh-e kashi, Shafii Kadkani

Floral Patterns on a Tile

Watercolour
77 x 54 cm
2007
Private collection

My thankfulness is to this white
poplar tree
my thankfulness is to all leaves in
their waking.

Awake all the night in their hope
of the dawning
in the hope of the sight of the sun
in the morning.

Excerpt from *Thankfulness*
Sepas, Shafii Kadkani

Thankfulness

Watercolour, acrylic ink
52 x 72 cm
2007
Private collection

Is there anyone
        who would ponder the thoughts of
the flowers
        red and azure
in the mirror of the stream at dawn?

Excerpt from
The Sacred Song of the Chrysanthemum
Mazameer-e gol-e davoudi
Shafii Kadkani

The Sacred Song of the Chrysanthemum

Watercolour
54 x 84 cm
2008
Private collection

How joyful such a bird as this
which is the poet of the garden's birds
which makes its home in flying
and makes its living singing

Excerpt from *Green on Green*
Sabz dar sabz, Shafii Kadkani

Green on Green

Watercolour, acrylic ink
76 x 40 cm
2008
Private collection

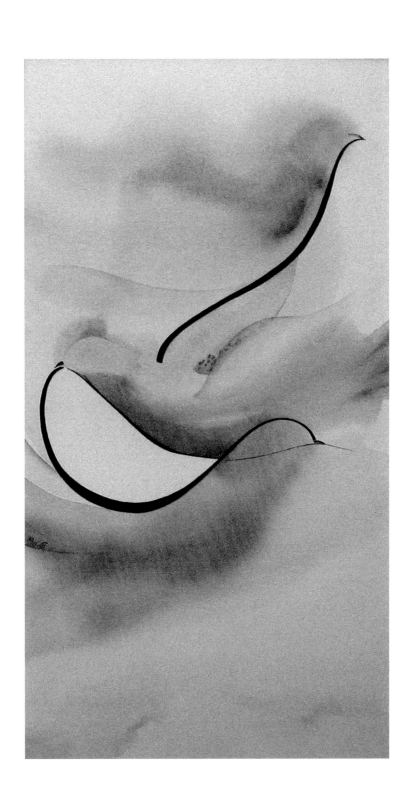

Look over there at those white poplars
they are sleeping yet awake
under the mantle of snow, and the sheet-glass of ice,
the life concealed
from the freezing breath of the winter months…

Excerpt from *The White Poplars*
Sepidaran, Shafii Kadkani

The White Poplars

Watercolour, acrylic ink
70 x 52 cm
2008
Private collection

The withered hand of winter
has stolen all the colours from this garden
such that in disconcertment you will say,
'In this place
there never was a garden or a spring.'

A Sketch in Charcoal
Siah ghalam, Shafii Kadkani

A Sketch in Charcoal

Watercolour, acrylic ink
75 x 30 cm
2008
Private collection

In the fearsome blowing and
buffeting of autumn
the sweetbrier, with its leaves and
branches
made a bridge
for the blossom to cross:
tomorrow's child.

Excerpt from
Of the Land of the Olive
Az sarzamin-e zeitoun
Shafii Kadkani

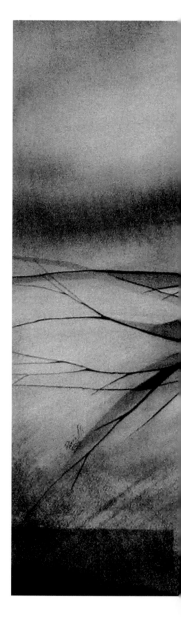

Of the Land of the Olive

Watercolour, acrylic ink
40 x 77 cm
2008
Private collection

Before you and me there were many who imprinted
the wall of life with such souvenirs.

This melody of tenderness will play on after you and me
for as long as the song of the rain and the wind endures in this world.

Excerpt from *Even with Time*
Hatta beh rouzgaran, Shafii Kadkani

Even with Time

Watercolour
68 x 50 cm
2009
Private collection

In truth could one
go and not stay?
In truth could one
recite a poem in praise
            of the poppies?

Excerpt from *In Truth Could One?*
Rasti aya? Shafii Kadkani

In Truth Could One?

Watercolour, acrylic ink
122 x 74 cm
2010
Private collection

The fragile hesitation of the night
is broken by the bird's wings
the shattering sound
of breaking glass is heard.
Once again, with the wailing sound of the
spreading wings
the veins of the garden are beating
are awakening.

Excerpt from *Birds Brimful of Dawn*
Parandegan-e por az sobh
Shafii Kadkani

Birds Brimful of Dawn

Watercolour, acrylic Ink
20 x 30.5 cm
2010
Private collection

The clusters of brushwood
and grasses
those, closest to the heart
of the earth
much earlier
have felt in their being
the sharp green taste of spring.

Excerpt from *Intuition*
Eshragh, Shafii Kadkani

Intuition

Watercolour, acrylic ink, 24k gold leaf
72 x 125 cm
2010
Private collection

Which season am I standing in?
On a shore
before my eyes
the springtime of green flames
the sparrows and the song
to your perception
bluish-grey and smoky.

Excerpt from *Which Season?*
Dar koja-ye fasl? Shafii Kadkani

Which Season?

Watercolour, acrylic ink
73 x 126 cm
2010
Artist's collection

No one would believe it!
See love's alchemy
see light's alchemy that turns
the tired earth
to morning greenness.

Excerpt from *Love's Green Alchemy*
Kimiya-ye sabz-e eshq
Shafii Kadkani

Love's Green Alchemy

Watercolour, acrylic ink
72 x 124 cm
2010
Artist's collection

I said of what use is this flapping, in such tight quarters
your wings getting tired?

They responded
and with a joyful scream
'We fly here, as we fear
that one day, we will forget our flight.'

Excerpts from *The Finches*
Fenj ha, Shafii Kadkani

The Finches

Watercolour, acrylic ink
74 x 45 cm
2010
Private collection

The first songbird of the garden
at the instance of blooming and utterance
on the highest branch of the garden, suddenly
erupts into its full throated song.

And then, exuberance and fervour in the garden
each bird bursting into flight with a song.

Excerpt from *In the Manner of the Morning*
Dar soluk-e sobh, Shafii Kadkani

In the Manner of the Morning

90 x 57 cm
Watercolour, acrylic ink
2010
Artist's collection

There, see that oak tree
half autumn and half spring.
It is as if the sorcery of autumn
has gone, arduously
up the trunk of the tree and from there
could not go any higher.

Excerpt from *In the Realm of Autumn*
Dar eqlim-e paeez, Shafii Kadkani

In the Realm of Autumn

Watercolour, acrylic ink, 24k gold leaf
123 x 75 cm
2010
Artist's collection

A day came when my thirst took away my patience
but when with passion and fervour, I raised my hand towards it
instead of pomegranate seeds
dark smoke and a demon jumped out
plunging the whole world into greyness.

Excerpt from *Pomegranate Garden*
Bagh-e anar, Shafii Kadkani

Pomegranate Garden

Watercolour, acrylic ink
93 x 58 cm
2010
Artist's collection

Oh creeping autumns
seeping into the green veins of the garden
such that our greenness is the arena of your thundering footsteps.

We are of a different species, a different spring.
We begin from the place where you end.

Beginning and End
Aghaz va payan, Shafii Kadkani

Beginning and End

Watercolour, acrylic
102 x 66 cm
2011
Artist's collection

A ladder is this life!
With steps that are numbered
from the first
to the highest
and we on our journey on these steps
are sometimes up
              sometimes down
each of us with an inevitable step
for himself
             from where
he travels towards the boundless.

Excerpt from *Ladder*
Nardeban, Shafii Kadkani

Ladder

Watercolour, acrylic
102 x 70 cm
2012
Private collection

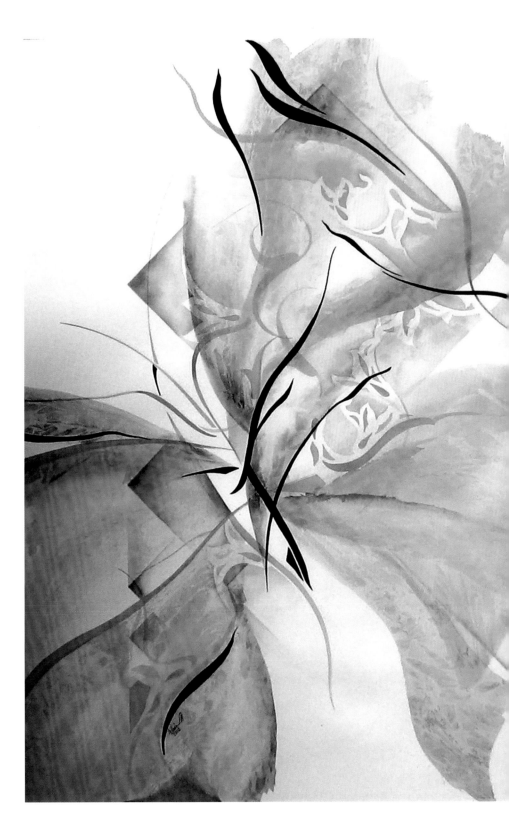

Beyond this cage, do you
breathe a breath of life?
Or the source of your existence
and your life am I?

Excerpt from *Dove
Kaboutar*, Shafii Kadkani

Dove

Watercolour
Diptych, each panel 95 x 44 cm
Both together, 95 x 88 cm
2012
Artist's collection

The moment the dark night of history spread its wings
look over there
the boundless abundance of sorrow!
Oh!

Excerpt from *Crows*
Zaghan, Shafii Kadkani

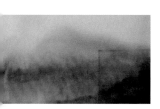

Crows

See following pages for descriptions

Crows Over the Garden

Watercolour, acrylic
48 x 107 cm
2012
Artist's collection

Crows Over the Window

Watercolour
85 x 85 cm
2012
Artist's collection

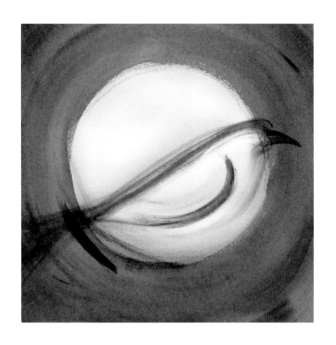

Crows Over the Moon

Watercolour, acrylic
48 x 48 cm
2012
Private collection

Crows Over the Snow

Watercolour, acrylic
48 x 48 cm
2012
Private collection

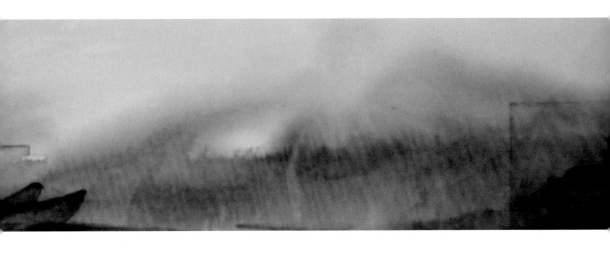

Crows Over the Path

Watercolour
20 x 107 cm
2012
Private collection

In a vase, on the table there is a flower
a gift from a beloved friend.

Red, fresh and full of life
as the morning mien of youth.

One can see it and be filled with joy
one can see it and be filled with thought

that finally it will wither
and will end up in a heap of litter.

Beyond these two there is no other way
depends on how you choose to see.

Flowers in a Vase
Golhay-e goldan, Shafii Kadkani

Flowers in a Vase

Watercolour
102 x 70 cm
2012
Artist's collection

The era of doubt and doubt in one's being
the era of doubt and doubt in one's doubt
the era of screaming in silence.

Excerpt from *On a Spider's Web*
Rouy-e tar-e ankabout, Shafii Kadkani

On a Spider's Web

Watercolour, acrylic
102 x 70 cm
2012
Private collection

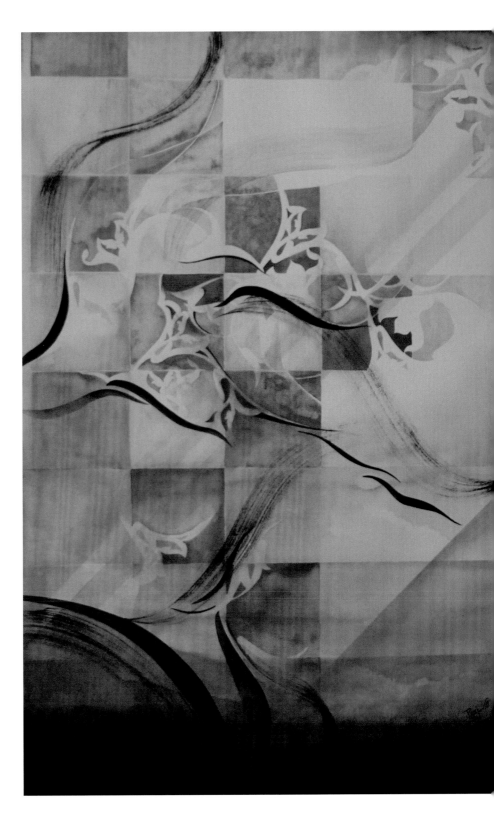

It is you who have
discovered the fifth
dimension of the tree.

*The Fifth Dimension
of the Tree
Buod-e panjom-e derakht
Shafii Kadkani*

*The Fifth Dimension
of the Tree
See following pages
for descriptions*

The Fifth Dimension of the Tree (1)

Watercolour, acrylic
43 x 30 cm
2012
Artist's collection

The Fifth Dimension of the Tree (2)

Watercolour, acrylic
43 x 30 cm
2012
Artist's collection

The Fifth Dimension of the Tree (3)

Watercolour, acrylic
57 x 72 cm
2012
Private collection

The Fifth Dimension of the Tree (4)

Watercolour, acrylic
30 x 30 cm
2012
Private collection

The Fifth Dimension of the Tree (5)

Watercolour, acrylic
30 x 30 cm
2012
Private collection

What is the name of this tree?
What is the name of this fortunate tree?

Excerpt from *The Name of this Tree*
Nam-e in derakht
Shafii Kadkani

The Name of this Tree

Watercolour, acrylic
70 x 120 cm
2012
Artist's collection

Art tells me: Do not be grieved, oh poet
as this meaning will not endure.

No status and setting will survive
if not in a rhythm desired by mankind.

If you remain, bring it to another rhythm
for the 'world', initiate another image.

An image, in which a humankind with new ideals
is brought forth, free of animosity.

And if you leave and this rhythm remains
do not be grieved by this misfortune and disloyalty.

After you other poets will come
and will compose it in the desired rhythm.

Excerpt from *The Rhythm of the 'World'*
Vazn-e 'jahan', Shafii Kadkani

Rhythm of the 'World'

See following pages for descriptions

Rhythm of the 'World' (1)

Watercolour, acrylic
50 x 76 cm
2012
Artist's collection

Rhythm of the 'World' (2)

Watercolour, acrylic
50 x 76 cm
2012
Artist's collection

Rhythm of the 'World' (3)

Watercolour, acrylic
50 x 76 cm
2012
Artist's collection

Rhythm of the 'World' (4)

Watercolour, acrylic
50 x 76 cm
2012
Artist's collection

O, You, whose name is the highest of all
talk to us, once again
without a saviour, a mediator, or a message.

Excerpt from *As with the Almond Blossom*
An saan ke ba shokoufeh badaam, Shafii Kadkani

As with the Almond Blossom

Watercolour, acrylic
78 x 35 cm
2013
Private collection

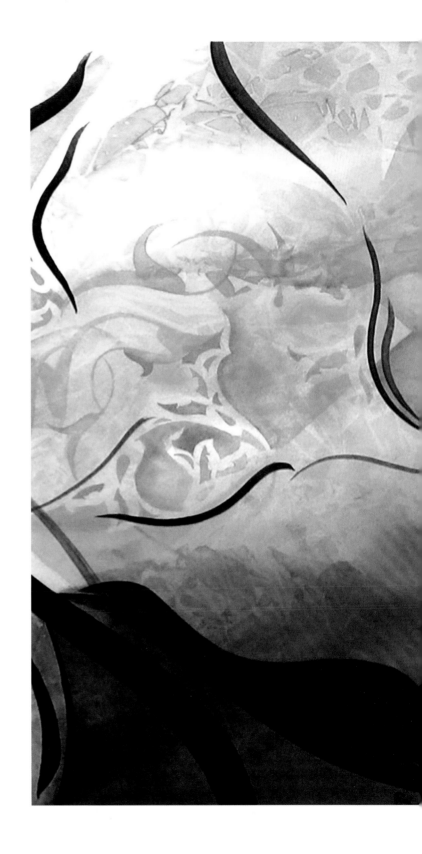

O You, from whom, emanates the light of our heart
the light of our sight
the turning of our awakened insight.

O You, from whom, arises winter, flourishes spring
from whom night turns into day, day into night.

O You, who alter our dispositions, our years,
make our disposition the most auspicious of all.

Nowruz Prayer, Shafii Kadkani

Auspicious Disposition

Watercolour, acrylic ink
103 x 87 cm
2016
Artist's collection

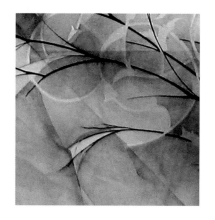

Painting the sound of the footsteps of water
inspired by a poem of Sohrab Sepehri

■ I am in Tehran
in the green summer of 2009.

I do not know why I am reading
The Sound of the Footsteps of Water
Sohrab Sepehri's long and well-known poem
written some forty years before.

Sohrab seems to be a witness to all this
observing the green vast landscape of light
and the spreading darkness
his gaze on the bigger picture
his calm voice
talking about unity
equality and freedom.

> The people, I saw.
> The cities, I saw.
> The plains, the mountains, I saw.
> Water I saw, earth, I saw.
> Light and darkness I saw.
> Plants I saw in light, and plants I saw in darkness.
> Animals I saw in light, and animals I saw in darkness.
> And humans I saw in light, and humans I saw in darkness.

As I read the poem again and again
many lines stand out for me.
He talks of nature as a universal symbol
for spiritual contemplation.
He talks of the unity and beauty of existence
sanctity of freedom to choose
the need for acceptance and inclusion of all.

My *Qibla* is a red rose
my prayer mat the fountainhead
my prayer stone the light
the field my prayer rug.

In my prayer arises the moon
arises the rainbow.
Beyond my prayer
the rock is visible.
The particles of my prayer have all crystallized.

My prayers
I say
when the call to prayer is sung
by the wind
on the minaret of the cypress.
My prayers I say
when summoned by the grass
when beckoned by the wave.

In this house I am close to the humble humidity of the grass.
I hear the sound of the garden breathing
and the dark sound of oppression as it falls from a leaf.

Despite hearing the dark sound of oppression
his focus seems to be on the individual responsibility
to search for beauty and truth
longing for and promoting
equality and respect for all.

Perhaps our job is
to swim in the magic of the rose.

Perhaps our job is to take back
the names we have given to the cloud
to the plane tree
to mosquito
to summer.

Perhaps our job is
to run between the lotus flower and the century
in search of the song of truth.

Sepehri talks of life
the journey of his life
the peaks and the valleys
the dark and the light
and the wisdom gained in his life
the wisdom of patience
respect and responsibility.
I am motivated to convey
my experience of that poem
in the summer of 2009 in Tehran
in the language of my paintings
a personal and humble re-expression
of a timeless poem.

I began painting my interpretations of Sohrab Sepehri's poem in Tehran and continued to paint during the next several months in Vancouver creating thirty-six paintings expressing my perceptions of the various lines of the poem layered with my experiences of the events and ambiance of the 2009 summer in Tehran. The paintings were exhibited in Iran and Canada.

My *Qibla* is a red rose
my prayer mat the fountainhead
my prayer stone the light
the field, my prayer rug.

Excerpt from *The Sound of the Footsteps of Water*
Seday-e pay-e ab, Sohrab Sepehri

My Qibla is a Red Rose

Watercolour, acrylic ink
94 x 58.5 cm
2009
Artist's collection

My Ka'aba by the water.
My Ka'aba is under the acacias.
My Ka'aba, like the breeze
passes from garden to garden
passes from town to town.

Excerpt from *The Sound of the Footsteps of Water*
Seday-e pay-e ab, Sohrab Sepehri

My Ka'aba Under the Acacia Trees

Watercolour, acrylic ink
72 x 44 cm
2009
Private collection

My black stone is the light on the flowerbeds.

Excerpt from *The Sound of the Footsteps of Water*
Seday-e pay-e ab, Sohrab Sepehri

My Black Stone

Watercolour, acrylic ink, 24k gold leaf
72 x 44 cm
2009
Private collection

Our garden was where feeling and foliage coalesced.
Our garden was the merging point of perception
cage and mirror.
Our garden was
perhaps
an arc from the green circle of felicity.

Excerpt from *The Sound of the Footsteps of Water*
Seday-e pay-e ab, Sohrab Sepehri

Feeling and Foliage

Watercolour and acrylic ink
90 x 51 cm
2008
Private collection

The moment a pomegranate cracked, my hand became a fountain of desire.
The moment a sparrow sang, the heart burnt with the delight of hearing.

Excerpt from *The Sound of the Footsteps of Water*
Seday-e pay-e ab, Sohrab Sepehri

The Moment a Pomegranate Cracked

Watercolour, acrylic ink
79 x 52 cm
2009
Private collection

Life resembled rain in Nowruz, a sycamore full of starlings.
Life at that time was a line-up of light and dolls
was an armful of freedom.
Life at that time was a pond of music.

Excerpt from *The Sound of the Footsteps of Water*
Seday-e pay-e ab, Sohrab Sepehri

A Pond of Music

Watercolour, acrylic ink
92 x 58 cm
Artist's collection

The battle of an opening with the pleading of the light
the battle of one step with the tall leg of the Sun
the battle of loneliness with a song.

Excerpt from *The Sound of the Footsteps of Water*
Seday-e pay-e ab, Sohrab Sepehri

The Pleading of Light

Watercolour, acrylic ink and 24k gold leaf
94 x 58 cm
2009
Private collection

I saw light and darkness.
I saw plants in light and plants in darkness.
I saw beasts in light and beasts in darkness.
I saw man in light and man in darkness.

Excerpt from *The Sound of the Footsteps of Water*
Seday-e pay-e ab, Sohrab Sepehri

Light and Darkness

Watercolour, acrylic ink
Seven panels: Each 43 x 27 cm
2009
Private collection

I am a native of Kashan, but
Kashan is not my city.
My city is lost.
With fortitude, with fervour
I have built another home on the other side of the night.

Excerpt from *The Sound of the Footsteps of Water*
Seday-e pay-e ab, Sohrab Sepehri

My City Is Lost

Watercolour and acrylic ink
90 x 58 cm
2009
Private collection

In this house I am close to the humble humidity of the grass.
I hear the sound of the garden breathing
and the dark sound of oppression as it falls from a leaf
and the sound of luminescence coughing behind a tree
sneezing of water in every crevice of the rock.

Excerpt from *The Sound of the Footsteps of Water*
Seday-e pay-e ab, Sohrab Sepehri

The Sound of the Garden Breathing (1)

Watercolour, acrylic ink, 24k gold leaf
94 x 58.5 cm
2009
Private collection

The Sound of the Garden Breathing (2)

Watercolour, acrylic ink, 24k gold leaf
94 x 59 cm
2009
Private collection

The Sound of the Garden Breathing (3)

93 x 58 cm
Watercolour, acrylic ink, 24k gold leaf
2009
Artist's collection

The Sound of the Garden Breathing (4)

Watercolour, acrylic ink, 24k gold leaf
94 x 58.5 cm
2009
Private collection

The Sound of the Garden Breathing (5)

Watercolour, acrylic ink, 24k gold leaf
93 x 57 cm
2009
Private collection

I am close to the beginning of the earth.
I feel the pulse of the flowers.
I am conscious of the wet destiny of water
and the green habit of the tree.

Excerpt from *The Sound of the Footsteps of Water*
Seday-e pay-e ab, Sohrab Sepehri

The Pulse of the Flowers

Watercolour, acrylic ink
94 x 59 cm
2009
Artist's collection

Life is about living in the pool of 'Now'.

Excerpt from *The Sound of the Footsteps of Water*
Seday-e pay-e ab, Sohrab Sepehri

Living in the Pool of 'Now'

Watercolour, acrylic ink
Seven panels, each 27 x 27 cm
2009
Artist's collection

Behind us, the bird is not singing.
Behind us the wind is not blowing.
Behind us the green window of spruce is closed.
Behind us there is the weariness of history.

Excerpt from *The Sound of the Footsteps of Water*
Seday-e pay-e ab, Sohrab Sepehri

The Fin Garden, Weariness of History

Watercolour, acrylic ink
91 x 51 cm
2008
Private collection

It is not our job to unravel the mystery of the rose.
Our job is perhaps to be immersed in the magic of the rose.

Excerpt from *The Sound of the Footsteps of Water*
Seday-e pay-e ab, Sohrab Sepehri

The Mystery of the Rose

Watercolour
94 x 60 cm
2009
Artist's collection

Perhaps our job is to
take back the names
we have given
to the cloud
to the plane tree
to the mosquito
to summer
to climb the height of
affection on the wet
legs of rain
to open the door
to mankind
to light
to plants
to insects.

Excerpt from
*The Sound of the
Footsteps of Water
Seday-e pay-e ab,*
Sohrab Sepehri

Nameless

Watercolour, acrylic ink
Triptych, each panel
94 x 60 cm
2009
Artist's collection

Perhaps our job is to run between the lotus flower and the century
in search of the song of truth...

Excerpt from *The Sound of the Footsteps of Water*
Seday-e pay-e ab, Sohrab Sepehri

In Search of the Song of Truth

Watercolour, acrylic ink
93 x 60 cm
2009
Artist's collection

The ambitious unfinished project of painting the
poems of Hafez

■ It was the summer of year 2006.
In a room with a glass door
opening onto a small brick walled garden with pink geraniums
I studied the poetry of Hafez
every morning for three months
with a mentor Alireza Heydari
a prominent writer-publisher in Tehran.

Like many Iranians
he had a lifelong love of the poetry of Hafez
knew the complete *Divan* by heart
recited the poems at every occasion
and had the dream of publishing
a new illustrated volume of Hafez.

For him the visual interpretations
in the existing published volumes did not convey
the complex beauty and wisdom of the poems.
He spoke of the *ghazals* with reverence and respect:

'The poetry of Hafez
can guide us to the awareness
of a special sense of sight
a certain way of seeing the world
endowing us with the ability
to truly appreciate the beauty of existence.

To know the beauty of existence
is to be close to the creator of beauty
a long path with no end
continuously bringing us closer
to a deeper understanding and appreciation of life.'

He gave me the opportunity to study with him
to understand and connect with Hafez
to create paintings inspired by the poems
for the new volume that would be his offering
to the poet he so loved
and to the lovers of Hafez everywhere.

He saw the poetry of Hafez
and its vast multi-faceted dimensions and meanings
in a new abstract contemporary visual language
rooted in the rich symbolic repository of Persian art.

In the room overlooking the garden
with the pink geraniums
we studied one hundred and twenty *ghazals* of Hafez
discussed the historical and social context
contemplated the language and multi-layered messages
praised the beauty and wisdom of the poems.

I had hardly begun to understand.
Painting this work would be a dream and a challenge.

Inspired and excited
with the idea of experimenting
and developing a visual language
for the expression of these timeless poems
I came back to my studio in Vancouver
and began to paint a small selection of the poems.
The plan was that with the completion of these paintings
and his review and comments
we would continue the study of Hafez
and I would resume the painting of more poems.

A year later eleven paintings were completed.
Unsure of my endeavours
wanting to know his views
I sent the photographs to Tehran
with a letter asking for his comments
stating that the paintings were only explorations
some perhaps fit only to be discarded.

Keen to know his views
I awaited impatiently for his response.
Two weeks passed.

He never saw the paintings.

A few days before he was to receive the photographs
he suffered a massive heart attack on a hiking trip
on the slopes of the magnificent Alborz range.
He lost his life in the landscape he so loved
leaving his family and friends
and many unfinished projects behind.

I was in total shock
disbelief and grief for a long time
deeply saddened and depressed
with the loss of a friend and mentor.

With his loss
I could not continue with the project.

As a remembrance and as symbols of my gratitude to my mentor, eleven paintings depicting my interpretations of specific lines from eleven *ghazals* of Hafez were exhibited in Tehran in 2009.

Speak of the minstrel and the wine
and seek not the mystery of the universe
since no one has unlocked
and no one will unlock
this riddle through wisdom.

Excerpt from *ghazal* 3, Hafez
Natel-Khanlari Edition

Speak of the Minstrel and the Wine

Watercolour
72 x 50 cm
2007
Artist's collection

The mirror of Alexander is the cup of wine, look
for it can reveal for you the state of the country of Darius.

Excerpt from *ghazal 5*, Hafez
Natel-Khanlari Edition

The Mirror of Alexander

Watercolour
70 x 30 cm
Watercolour
2007
Artist's collection

In the feast of the cycle
drink a cup or two and leave.
Be aware not to crave
for an enduring connection.

Excerpt from *ghazal 7*, Hafez
Natel-Khanlari Edition

Drink a Cup or Two and Leave

Watercolour, acrylic ink
47 x 70 cm
2007
Artist's collection

Last night, our master came from the mosque to the tavern.
After this, companion wayfarers
what ought to be our acumen?

Excerpt from *ghazal* 10, Hafez
Natel-Khanlari Edition

From the Mosque to the Tavern

Watercolour
72 x 50 cm
2007
Artist's collection

Praise to the Divine
that this blast of autumnal wind did not pervade
your garden of jasmine, cypress, rose and boxwood.

Excerpt from *ghazal* 19, Hafez
Natel-Khanlari Edition

This Blast of Autumnal Wind

Watercolour, acrylic ink
68 x 50cm
2007
Artist's collection

The moment I performed my ablutions in the fountain of love
I liberated myself, at once, of all that exists.

Excerpt from *ghazal* 21, Hafez
Natel-Khanlari Edition

Ablutions in the Fountain of Love

Watercolour
72 x 38 cm
2007
Private collection

Within me, the one with the battered heart
I do not know who resides
since I am silent and he is restless and flustered.

Excerpt from *ghazal* 26, Hafez
Natel-Khanlari Edition

Within Me

Watercolour
67 x 48 cm
2007
Artist's collection

In how many colours
did the cupbearer pour the wine in the cup?
See all these patterns
how beautifully they are cast on the marrow.

Excerpt from *ghazal* 32, Hafez
Natel-Khanlari Edition

See All These Patterns

Watercolour, acrylic ink
68 x 49 cm
2007
Private collection

Did the tulip know the infidelity of the world?
Since from birth to death
it did not put down the cup of wine.

Excerpt from *ghazal 97*, Hafez
Natel-Khanlari Edition

Did the Tulip Know?

Watercolour
72 x 47 cm
2007
Artist's collection

Last night a wise man whispered in my ear
He was learned from a divine and holy teacher
And said he would tell me his revelations if I drew near
I sat back to take in the words of this spiritual speaker.

He told me I should view life from a place of ease
For those who perceive the gift of life as a trial
All the splendor of the world will fail to please
But with open heart the hardest of tasks shall evoke a smile.

He set in front of me a glass of the reddest wine
Wherein its magical contents were so pure
As to invoke the presence of the Venus Divine
She sang to me that for all my woes she had the cure.

She said 'when your heart is bleeding from sorrow
As though pierced by the sharpest knife
But smile as wide as the mouth of the glass of wine that you borrow
And you will overcome the saddest of all human strife.'

As my intoxication subsided I saw the speaker with a sullen face
He said he realized that without experience I could not understand
For the knowledge of Heaven's Grace
Can only be learned by one with a practiced hand.

Excerpt from *ghazal* 281, Hafez
Natel-Khanlari Edition
Translated by Shirin Raz Yamini, 2006

When Your Heart is Bleeding from Sorrow

72 x 45 cm
Watercolour
2007
Private collection

My heart cut loose
and I
the dervish
am heedless
what came
upon that bewildered prey.

I ponder the patience
of the ocean.
Alas
what is this drop
contemplating
the impossible?

Excerpt from
ghazal 285, Hafez
Natel-Khanlari Edition

My Heart Cut Loose

Watercolour
41 x 71 cm
2007
Artist's collection

Painting the story of the city of stones
inspired by a poem of Akhavan Saless

■ The poem
a symbolic expression of the struggles of mankind
and specifically of Iranians for freedom
was written after the events of 1953
drawing from the symbolism of ancient Iran
Zoroastrian myths
and figures from ancient epic stories of *Shahnameh*.

It is a commentary on the continuing endless struggle
of Iranians for emancipation.
The poem tells the story
of a wandering distressed sovereign
and his city of stones
witnessed and narrated by two pigeons
on the branches of an old lotus tree.

Akhavan talks of the rich and glorious past
and contrasts it with the deteriorated situation
he witnesses in his society
and points to complex internal and external elements
causing the problems of *'The City of Stones'*.

It is a beautiful work of art with a rich symbolism
working in many layers of history and meaning.

I began to paint this poem in 2010. The two paintings completed to this day narrating the opening passages of *The Story of the City of Stones* are included in *My Blue Canvas*. Eight more panels to depict my understanding of the rest of the story are yet to be painted.

Two pigeons
are sitting on the branch of an old lotus tree
that has grown apart from its companions
on the skirts of the rugged mountain.

Two kind, congenial creatures together
two sad storytellers of their shared sorrows together
how pleasant, yes, how pleasant is the bond
of two souls of one tongue together.

Excerpt from *The Story of the City of Stones*
Gheseh shahr-e sangestan, Akhavan Saless

Two Pigeons on the Old Lotus Tree

Watercolour, acrylic ink
148 x 96 cm
2010
Artist's collection

You didn't say, sister dearest, this person lying here, who he is.

Distressed, estranged, wearied, lost on his way, he seems
a shepherd, his flocks devoured by wolves
or else a merchant, his goods swallowed by the sea
and perhaps a lover, bewildered across mountains and deserts.
He has surrendered his heart to a dream
no peace does he attain from repose
no peace from crossing the ocean
the mountain
the plain and the field.

Excerpt from *The Story of the City of Stones*
Gheseh shahr-e sangestan, Akhavan Saless

The Sovereign of the City of Stones

Watercolour, acrylic ink
148 x 96 cm
2010
Artist's collection

Art in precious metals
Games, Jewellery, Furniture

My journey of working with precious metals
was initiated in the year 1992
by our younger son.
Having seen the artwork
and handmade jewellery of a friend's mother
he wanted to see if I could also
learn to work in the exciting medium
of precious metals
and was urging me to try.

During the previous eight years
since 1984
I had been painting my memories of Persian gardens
inspired by the poetry of Omar Khayyam.

A Survey of Persian Art
edited by Arthur Upham Pope and Phyllis Ackerman
published in 1938
an important reference book for me
during my years
at the school of architecture in Tehran
had once again become
my inspiring reference book in Vancouver.

I spent hours reading the text
contemplating the photographs and drawings
of monuments and gardens
carpets and textiles
miniature paintings
manuscript illuminations
works in metal
pottery and faience.

The order
the unity and simplicity
the sophistication and complexity
of the ideas and aesthetic sensibilities
in so many different genres of artistic creation
are impressive and inspiring.
This is my artistic lineage
I thought
with respect and deep humility.

The works in metal attracted my attention
brass bowls and pen boxes
scissors and rulers
watch cases and belt buckles
incense burners and astrolabes
pierced and engraved
inlaid with gold and silver
everyday items transformed into
works of timeless beauty and intricacy
in the hands of unknown master craftsmen.

Our son's fascination with
crafting everyday items out of precious metals
took me again to the pages of the book
and the creations of Persian artists and craftsmen of centuries past.
His deeply felt and expressed enthusiasm
at such a young age
for the idea of creating beautiful artefacts
gave me the courage to begin and set me
on a most fulfilling journey
learning the art and craft
of creating pieces in precious metals.

Enrolling in a two-year full time course
I began the exciting exploration
of working with precious metals
learning the techniques
of making hand-crafted jewellery
a challenging and transforming experience.

Ideas of rules and regulations
boundaries and frameworks
in relation to spontaneity and freedom
in life and in art
had been a constant concern and focus of exploration
in my paintings.
The options for exploration
of such concepts in painting were endless
unlimited colours and textures
free flowing lines and geometric patterns
the interplay and tensions between them
communicating complex issues
in the non verbal language of my art.

With the very limited pallet of works in metal
white and oxidised sterling silver
subtle shades of gold
and hard to achieve textures
this exploration was more challenging
but not impossible.
I designed and crafted a backgammon game
in sterling silver and gold *keum-boo*
to explore these ideas
to use the medium of precious metals
for the contemplation and expression of abstract concepts.

The goal that inspired and drove me
to carry out the challenging work
was experimenting with the motifs
of traditional Persian art
adopting and simplifying them
within a contemporary concept of design.
The aim was to use the medium of precious metals
and the potentials of those timeless motifs
not just for the creation of decorative pieces
but as a medium for complex and multi-layered
artistic expression.

Two years later I entered a DeBeers competition
Beyond Tradition
for the design of a piece of jewellery
using diamonds and a non-traditional material.
I submitted a design for a chess set
thirty-two playing pieces of Plexiglas
with pierced and soldered gold caps
set with diamonds
riveted with gold pins
onto the Plexiglas bases
chess pieces wearable as rings
standing on a sandblasted glass chess board.

I won the design competition
and committed to completing the creation
of the thirty-two piece set in sixteen weeks.
The work was demanding
had to be perfect
was exciting and challenging
involving several rounds of melting and remaking.

Working non-stop sixteen-hour days on the bench
for the full sixteen weeks
my neck in a brace
I finished the thirty-two piece chess set
in time for a year-long exhibition tour
in major Canadian cities.

Creating and exhibiting other games
became an exciting and fulfilling involvement
backgammon games
snakes and ladders
tangrams and puzzles
as well as other chess sets
in precious metals
all inspired by motifs and elements
from the vast treasury of Persian art.
Many lifetimes could be spent working with these motifs
never just copying the traditional design
but interpreting and expressing them
within a contemporary design context and sensibility.

I designed and created several games
as parts of fundraising exhibitions
to benefit among others
the *Encyclopaedia Iranica*
the victims of the Bam earthquake
and the Vancouver Symphony Orchestra.

The richness and versatility of the repertoire of Persian art is endless. With a focus on understanding the aesthetic sensibilities and the inherent geometric order of the forms, and without the need to exactly copy any existing motif, the artist can create unique and timeless pieces. My designs of the games in precious metals and the jewellery are just one interpretation of the multitudes of possibilities.

Checkers Set

Sterling silver square board inserts
Acid-etched and oxidised geometric motifs
Jade and carnelian cabochon checkers
Sandblasted and carved glass board
30 x 30 x 0.9 cm
1992
Artist's collection

Chess Set

Hand-pierced sterling silver board inserts wearable as pendants
Sterling silver game pieces with 18k gold motifs
Wearable as rings
Sandblasted and carved glass board
31 x 31 x 0.9 cm
1993
Artist's collection

Chess Set

Winner of DeBeers Award, *Beyond Tradition*, 1994
Chess pieces
Wearable as rings in colourless transparent and black Plexiglas
18k gold hand-pierced covers
Set with a total of two carats of diamonds
Sandblasted glass board
47 x 47 x 0.9 cm
1994
Artist's collection

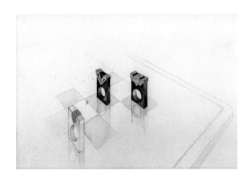
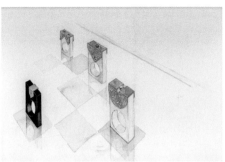

Chess Set

Chess pieces wearable as rings
Colourless transparent and smoky Plexiglas
14k gold hand-pierced covers set with jade and lapis lazuli
Sandblasted glass board
45 x 45 x 0.9 cm
1994
Artist's collection

Details of playing pieces
King and Queen
Wearable as rings

Backgammon Set

Board inserts of hand-pierced, textured sterling silver and18k gold
Wearable as pendants and earrings
Checkers of green jade and pink rhodonite cabochons
Hematite dice
Sandblasted and carved black granite board with raised edges
51 x 51 x 2 cm
1995
Artist's collection

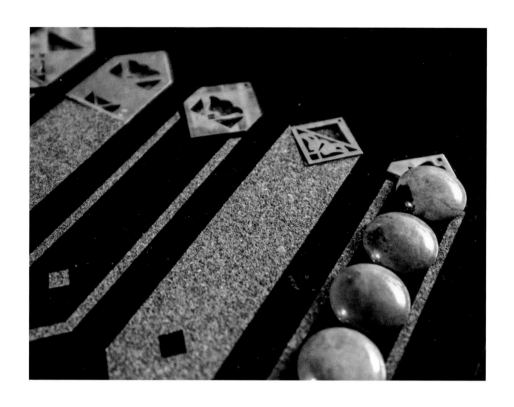

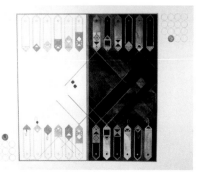

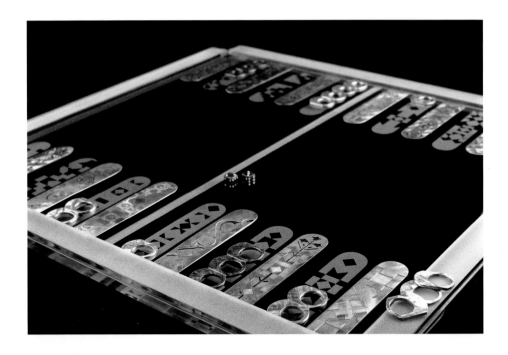

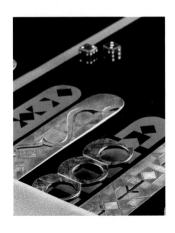
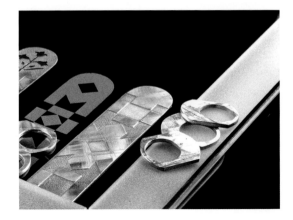

Backgammon Set

Sterling silver board inserts wearable as pendants
Hand-pierced and textured
With 18k gold motifs and 24k gold *keum-boo* motifs
Checkers of sterling silver with 24k gold *keum-boo* motifs
Wearable as rings
Sandblasted and carved glass board with raised edges
41 x 41 x 2 cm
1994
Private collection

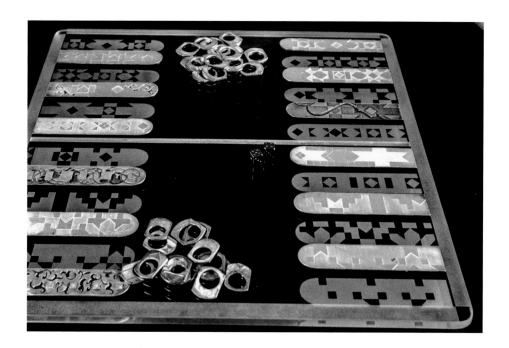

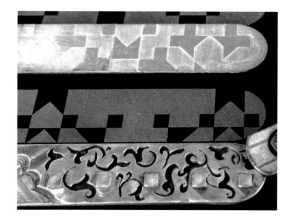

Backgammon Set

Sterling silver board inserts wearable as pendants
Hand-pierced and textured with 18k gold motifs
and 24k gold *keum-boo* motifs
Checkers of sterling silver
with 24k gold *keum-boo* motifs wearable as rings
Sandblasted and carved glass board
39.5 x 39.5 x 0.9 cm
1995
Artist's collection

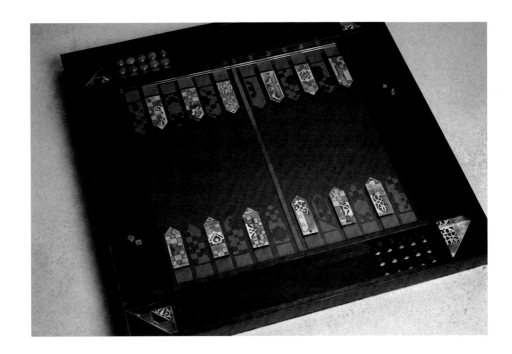

Backgammon Set

Sterling silver board inserts wearable as pendants
Hand-pierced acid-etched, oxidised, 24k gold *keum-boo* motifs
Sterling silver hand-pierced corner pieces wearable as pendants
Green jade and pink rhodonite cabochon checkers
Sandblasted and carved glass board, 43 x 43 x 0.9 cm
Walnut box with ebony motifs, 60 x 60 x 5 cm
1995
Private collection

Iranica Backgammon Set

Sterling silver board inserts wearable as pendants
Hand-pierced acid-etched, oxidised, 24k gold *keum-boo* motifs
Sterling silver hand-pierced corner pieces wearable as pendants
Lapis Lazuli and carnelian cabochon checkers
Sandblasted and carved glass board, 43 x 43 x 0.9 cm
Walnut box with ebony motifs, 60 x 60 x 5 cm
1996
Artist's collection

Two Snakes and Ladders Sets

Sterling silver, 14k and 18k gold board inserts
Wearable as pendants and earrings
Playing pieces of semi-precious stones
Hand-pierced gold and sterling silver covers
Wearable as pendants
Sandblasted and carved glass boards
39.5 x 39.5 x 0.9 cm
42 x 42 x 0.9 cm
1994
Private collections

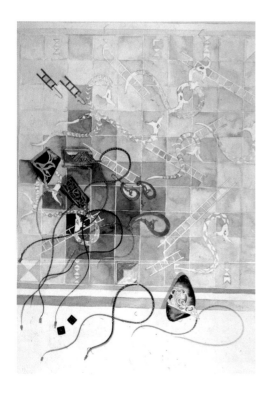

Snakes and Ladders Set

Sterling silver, 14k gold board inserts
Wearable as pendants and earrings
Playing pieces of semi-precious stones wearable as pendants
Hand-pierced gold and sterling silver covers
Sandblasted and carved glass board
30 x 30 x 0.9 cm
1995
Private collection

Snakes and Ladders Set

Sterling silver, 14k and 18k gold hand-pierced board inserts
Wearable as pendants and earrings
Playing pieces of semi-precious stones wearable as pendants
Hand-pierced gold and sterling silver covers
Sandblasted and carved glass boards
42 x 42 x 0.9 cm
1995
Artist's collection

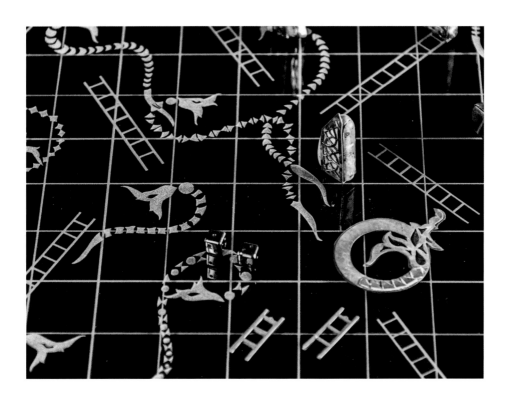

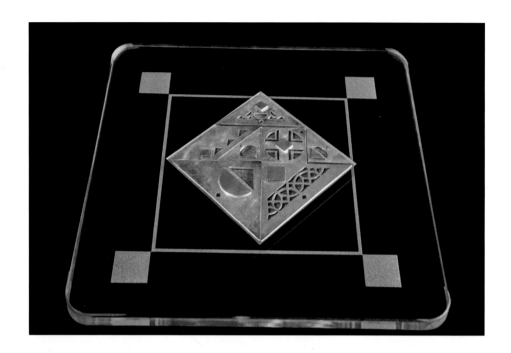

Two Sets of Tangram Puzzles

Sterling silver puzzle pieces wearable as pendants and earrings
Hand-pierced, acid-etched and oxidised
18k gold and 24k gold *keum-boo* motifs
Sandblasted and carved glass boards
2004
Artist's collection

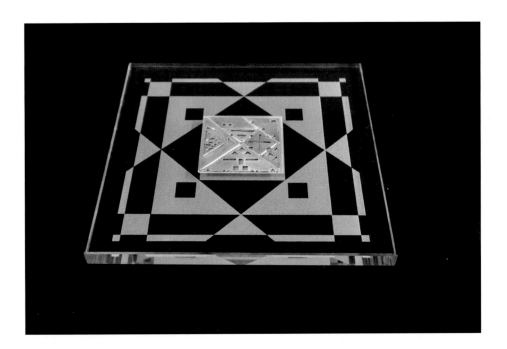

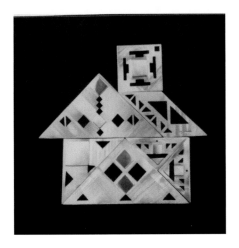

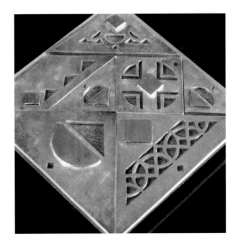

Various puzzle solutions
Combinations of seven tangram puzzle pieces in precious metals
Man, Horse, Rabbit, House

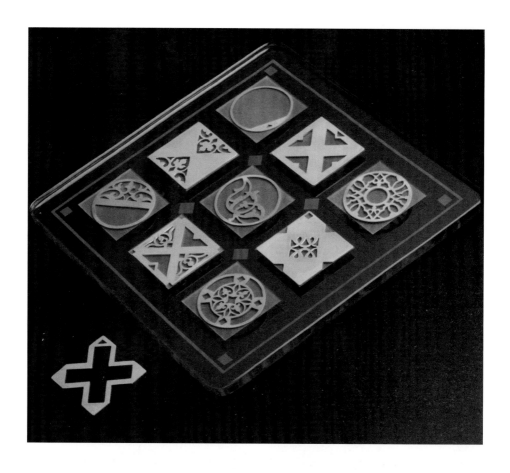

Three Sets of Tic-Tac-Toe Games

Sterling silver and 18k gold playing pieces
Wearable as pendants
Hand-pierced with 24k gold *keum-boo* motifs
Sandblasted and carved glass boards, various sizes
1997, 2001, 2004
Private and artist's collections

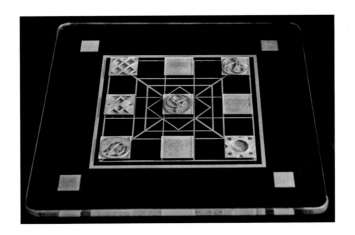

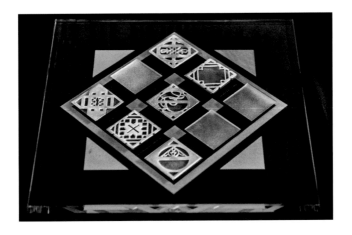

■ The beauty of the motifs
in the traditional Persian artistic heritage
motivated me to design and make pieces of jewellery
inspired by the traditional forms
but with a contemporary design sensibility.

A collection of jewellery was created
to fundraise for the *Encyclopaedia Iranica*.
The entire collection was inspired by the *Iranica* logo
and was exhibited in 1996 in New York city.

I created a collection of pieces with the words
'to love and be loved'
a few years
after the loss of our son
to honour his words
to keep me focused
to aspire to understand
what these words mean.

For the Museum of Anthropology in Vancouver
I created a collection inspired by the logo
of a 2001 exhibition
titled *The Spirit of Islam*.

To fundraise for the victims of the 2003 earthquake
in the city of Bam in Iran
I created another jewellery collection
which was exhibited in the year 2004 in Vancouver.

Necklaces, pendants, brooches, earrings, bookmarks, letter openers and paperweights all lend themselves to contemporary re-interpretation of traditional designs and motifs as presented in these pages of *My Blue Canvas*.

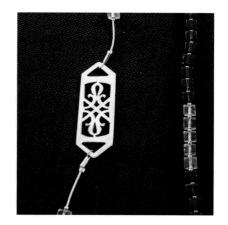

Necklaces

Hand-pierced sterling silver with 24k gold *keum-boo* motifs
Beads of semi-precious stones and pearls
1992–2004
Artist's and private collections

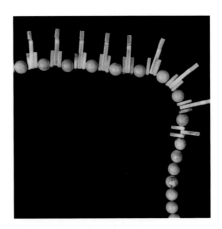

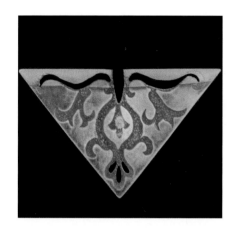

Necklaces

Hand-pierced sterling silver
24k gold *keum-boo* motifs
Strings of beads of semi-precious stones and leather
1992–2004
Artist's and private collections

Necklaces

Hand-pierced sterling silver
24k gold *keum-boo* motifs
Strings of jade, turquoise and pearl beads
1992–2004
Private collections

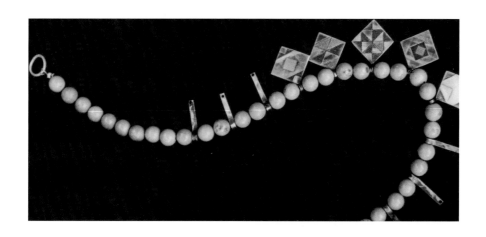

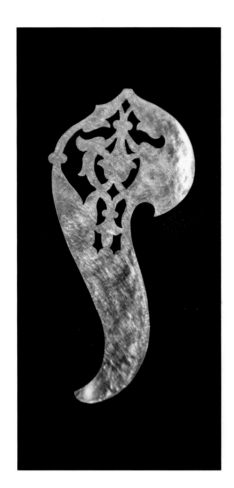

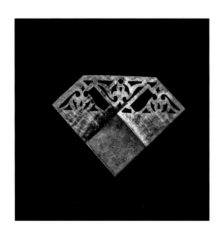

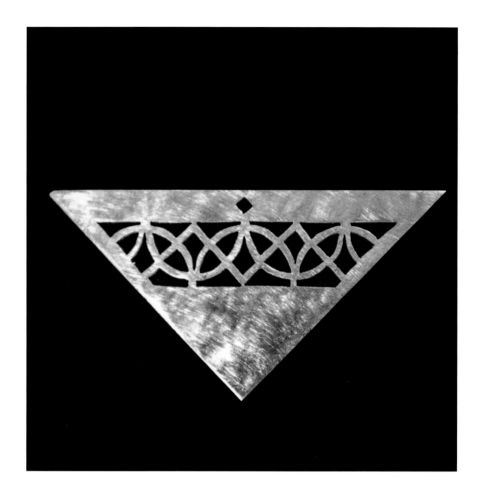

Pendants and Brooches

24k gold, textured and hand-pierced motifs
1992–2004
Artist's and private collections

Pendants

24k gold, hand-pierced and textured motifs
Gold chains or pearl strings
1992–2004
Artist's and private collections

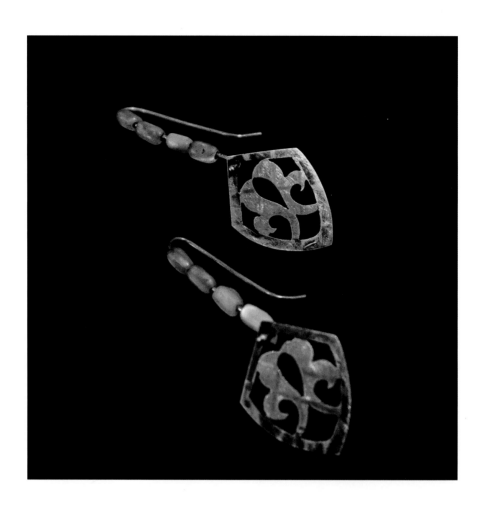

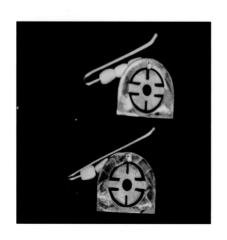

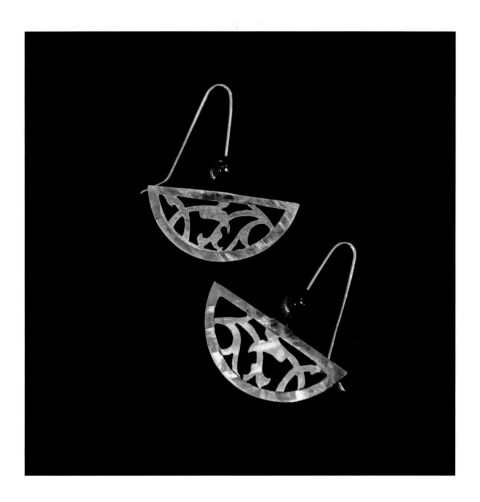

Earrings

Hand-pierced sterling silver, 24k gold *keum-boo* motifs
Lapis lazuli and mother-of-pearl beads
1992–2004
Artist's and private collections

'To love and be loved'
Pendants and Earrings

Hand-pierced sterling silver
Cast in rubber moulds and hand-finished
1999
Artist's and private collections

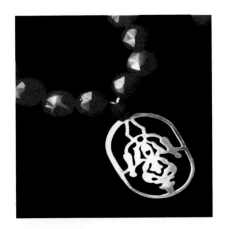

Pendants and Necklaces

Hand-pierced 24k gold, sterling silver pieces
Inspired by the *Encyclopaedia Iranica* logo
1996–1997
Private collections

Pendants and Brooches

Hand-pierced 24k gold set with
diamond, rubies, tourmaline and
amethyst stones
Inspired by
Encyclopaedia Iranica logo
1996–1997
Artist's and private collections

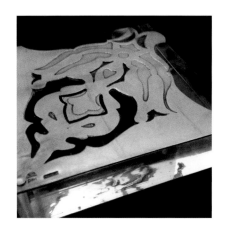
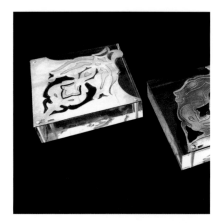

Paperweights

Hand-pierced sterling silver riveted on clear Plexiglas base
Inspired by the *Encyclopaedia Iranica* logo
1996–1997
Artist's and private collections

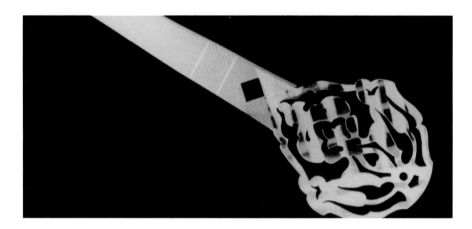

Letter Openers

Hand-pierced sterling silver polished and matte-textured
Inspired by the *Encyclopaedia Iranica* Logo
1996–1997
Artist's and private collections

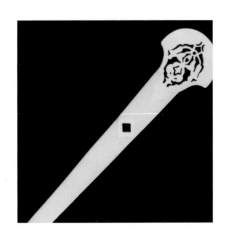

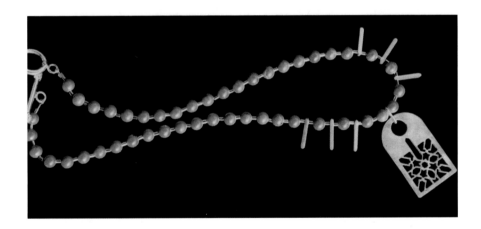

Pendants

Hand-pierced sterling silver pieces
Cast in a rubber mould and hand-finished
24k gold *keum-boo* motifs
Strings of semi-precious beads
Inspired by *The Spirit of Islam* Exhibition logo
Museum of Anthropology, Vancouver
2001
Artist's and private collections

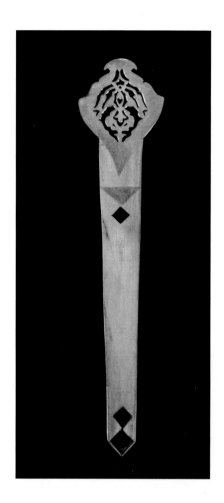

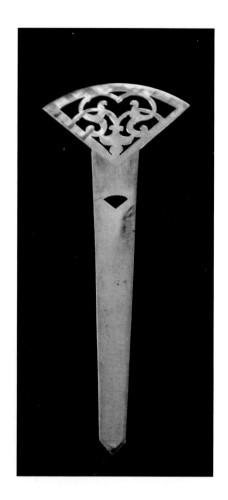

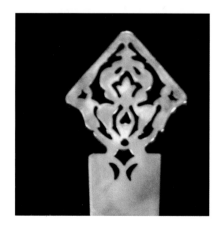

Letter Openers and Book Marks

Hand-pierced, textured
acid-etched and oxidised
sterling silver
24k gold *keum-boo* motifs
1994–1996
Artist's and private collections

■ Variations and possibilities for using motifs
from the repertoire of Persian visual art and crafts
in the design and creation of contemporary furniture seem endless.
For a short period I explored elements of this idea
and designed and created tables using these traditional motifs.

Wooden tables
with inlaid removable pierced sterling silver elements
with gold *keum-boo* motifs
topped with a sheet of thick glass
bring the ancient motifs
to a contemporary setting.

Simplified Persian artistic motifs and forms
come to life in a modern ambiance
as geometric or arabesque designs
on metal tables
covered with glass tops of various shapes
reminders of the timeless artistic sensibilities
of the master craftsmen who created them centuries before.

On the following pages a few examples of the tables are shown. My aim is to convey the versatility of traditional Persian motifs and the potential for new contemporary interpretations for use in many different contexts.

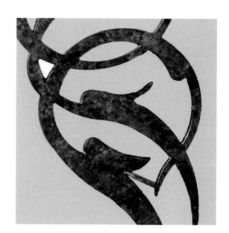

Persian Poem

Table in metal and glass
136 x 50 x 46.5 cm
2003

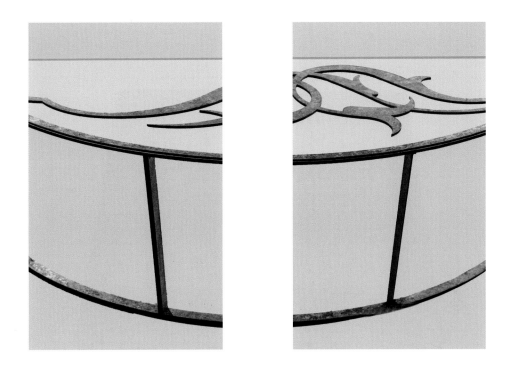

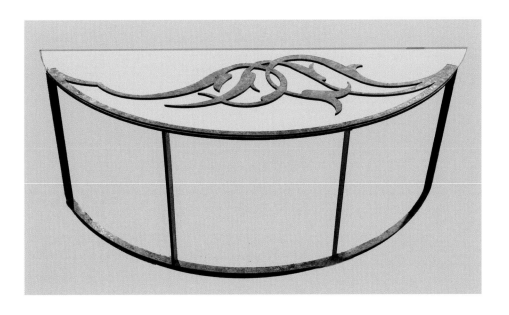

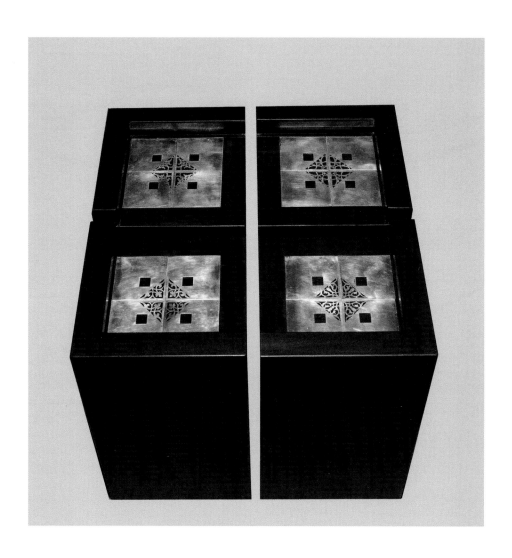

Persian Dream

Table in wood and glass
Removable hand-pierced sterling silver motifs
156 x 86 x 39.5 cm
1997

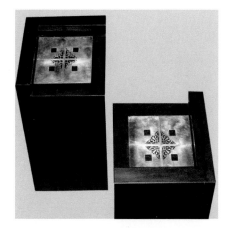

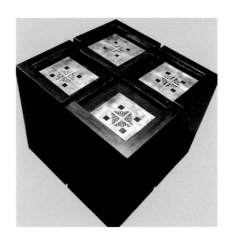

Persian Puzzle

Table in wood and glass with options for installation
Removable hand-pierced sterling silver and gold *keum-boo inserts*
152 x 52.5 x 53 cm
2003

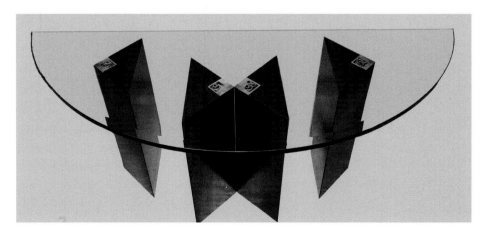

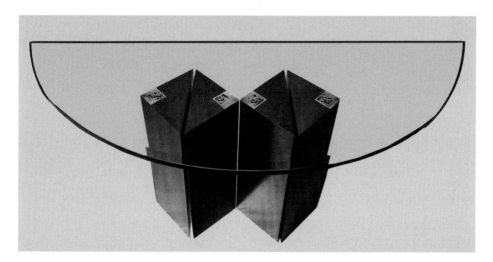

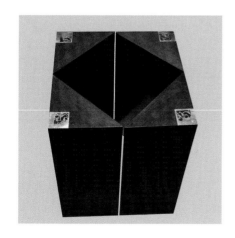

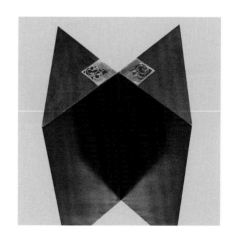

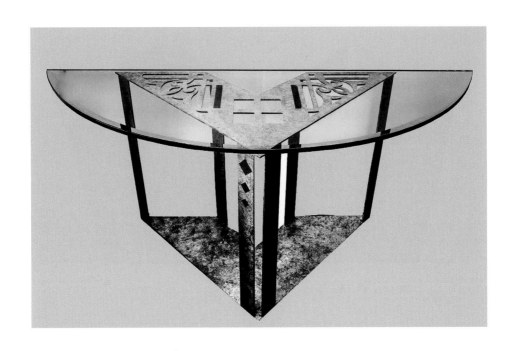

Persian Architecture

Table in metal and glass
186 x 61 x 78.5 cm
2003

Glossary

Ackerman, Phyllis (1893–1977): Author, editor, teacher and translator in the field of Oriental, European and Persian arts, iconography and symbolism. Ackerman and her husband Arthur Upham Pope published many books and articles on Iranian art including *A Survey of Persian Art from Prehistoric Times to the Present*.

Akhavan Saless, Mehdi (1928–1990): Prominent Iranian poet, editor and activist. His poems address social and political issues but also themes of love and nature, written in both classical and modern formats. An important poem, *Gheseh Shahr-e Sangestan*, or *The Story of the City of Stones*, published in the volume *Az in Avesta*, by Morvareed Publishers, Tehran, 1974, inspired two of the paintings in this book. Excerpts from the unpublished English translation of the poem by Pari Azarm Motamedi are included beside the paintings.

Ayvan: An important and influential feature of Iranian architecture since the Parthian period (250 BCE–226 CE). It is a single large vaulted hall walled on three sides and opening directly to the outside on the fourth. Sometimes it is also referred to as a palace or part of a palace.

Bibi joon: *Bibi* meaning 'lady' is a title originally reserved for high-ranking women and is of Turkic origin. It is also commonly applied to grandmothers and other elderly ladies in the family. *Joon* is a term of endearment in Persian.

Chahar Bagh: In Persian *chahar* means 'four' and *bagh* means 'garden'. Chahar Bagh is a rectangular garden layout, divided by walkways or flowing waterways into four symmetrical parts. This design has existed since the Achaemenid period and is evident at the royal gardens at Pasargadae near Persepolis in southern Iran, the ceremonial capital of the Persian Empire built in the 6th century BCE.

Courtyard House: An architectural form, which has existed in Iran and many parts of the world for thousands of years. It is a house with an inner courtyard: the walls or a building surround a private space or garden with rooms facing the courtyard. In the Islamic period the inner courtyards were often reserved for women and children, and only related males were allowed into this private space.

Cyrus the Great (600–530 BCE): Founder of the Achaemenid Dynasty and the first major world empire. Also known as the Persian Empire, at its peak the territories extended from India to Egypt. Cyrus is known in ancient sources as the first true statesman as he used diplomacy instead of force when possible, and ruled with tolerance, respecting diversity in cultures and religions.

Dowlatabad Garden: One of the nine gardens in Iran registered on the UNESCO list of World Heritage sites. The garden was built in the city of Yazd, in the 18th century for Karim Khan Zand, the founder of the Zand Dynasty.

Eram Garden: A registered world heritage site, this garden in Shiraz was built in the early nineteenth century for a tribal chief as his permanent residence. The garden is a public park, and in addition is used as a botanical garden by Shiraz University. *Eram* also means Paradise, and the name illustrates the beauty and tranquility of the garden.

Ferdowsi, Abu'l Qasem (940–1019 or 1025): The great Iranian epic poet and the author of the *Shahnameh, The Book of Kings*, the national epic of Iran. The book is the longest poem created by a single person, and contains around 50,000 verses. It is still very popular amongst Iranians.

Fin Garden and Bathhouse: Constructed by the Safavid monarch, Shah Safi (r. 1629–1642) repaired and added to in 1805 during the Qajar period. It served as the home of Amir Kabir, the exiled reformist Qajar prime minister, who lived in it for a short time and was assassinated in its bathhouse in 1852.

Ghazal: A lyric poem mostly on the theme of love. The Persian *ghazal* consists of a number of lines and statements that can be independent of each other. There is a repeated rhyme, and often the poems are set to music.

Hafez: Celebrated Persian lyric poet (1315–1390) whose book of poetry is found in most households in Iran. His poems greatly influenced post-fourteenth century Persian poetry. His poems are also used in divination, where questions are asked, wishes are made and poems read by opening the book randomly. The reader interprets the poem with regards to the question and the possibility of the wish becoming true. Excerpts from the eleven *ghazals* of Hafez depicted in *My Blue Canvas* were translated by the author from *Divan-e Hafez*, edited by Natel-Khanlari and published by Khawrazmi in Tehran in 1983. Shirin-Raz Yamini translated the excerpt of *ghazal* 281 into English.

Hasht Behesht: Meaning 'Eight gardens' is the name of an octagonal pavilion built in 1669–1670, in the *Bagh-e-Bolbol*, or Nightingale Garden in Isfahan during the reign of Shah Solayman of the Safavid Dynasty.

Heydari, Alireza: Publisher, writer and founder of Khawrazmi publishers in Iran, a pro-modernist publisher of books in arts, literature, philosophy and history.

Hijab: A loose female garment, prescribed by Islamic codes for covering the body, and sometimes the face.

Imshi: The name of a petroleum-based insect repellent that was used in Iran.

Jamshid's All Seeing Cup: A magical cup that allows the owner to see the unseen and forecast the future. Jamshid in the Ancient Zoroastrian text *Avesta* is known as Yima/Jam and has a ring and a cup with magical qualities. In *Shahnameh* he is a mythical king credited with many discoveries and innovations.

Isfahan: Ancient province and city in central Iran. One of the most important urban centres in Iran, with a population of 1.75 million in 2011, Isfahan is Iran's third largest city. UNESCO has designated many of Isfahan's monuments as World Heritage sites.

Kashan: Historical city in central Iran famous for its architecture. Inhabited since Neolithic times circa 6000 BCE, Kashan has been a major centre for production of ceramic ware for thousands of years.

Kelim: A floor covering similar to a carpet, produced since ancient times. It has tightly interwoven warp and weft, a flat surface and no pile.

Khosrow and Shirin: A famous romantic poem by Nezami Ganjavi (1141–1209), recounting the amorous relationship between the Sasanian king, Khosrow II Parviz, (r. 590–625 CE) and the beautiful Christian Princess, Shirin.

Korsi: A low table over a charcoal brazier. The table was covered with a large quilt and surrounded by mattresses for people to relax on. *Korsi* was a common feature in most Iranian homes during the winter months, until the late decades of the twentieth century.

Keum-boo: A popular technique in Asia since ancient times for binding thinly rolled gold foil to pure silver using heat and pressure to make silver-gilt.

Mangal: A metal brazier filled with coal, which was used for grilling, cooking and also for heating the traditional *korsi*.

Mashhad: Capital of Khorasan Province and the second largest city in Iran. Mashhad is located in the northeast of Iran and is home to the burial shrine of Imam Reza the 8th Shia imam. It had a population of around three million people in 2011.

Moshaereh: A game of poetry and memory played in Iran. One person recites a line from a poem; the next person must recite another line that begins with the last letter of the poem recited by the first person. If a person cannot remember a poem, she or he is excluded from the game. The last person that remains in the game is the winner.

Nezami Ganjavi (1141–1209): Iranian poet raised and buried in Ganjeh now in the Republic of Azerbaijan. The stories in his *Kamsa*, five narrative poems, including *Khosrow and Shirin*, have provided the Persian art of the miniature with an abundance of subject matter.

Nowruz: Meaning 'New Day' is an ancient pre-Islamic festival celebrating the Iranian New Year which is held on the first day of spring and marks the spring equinox usually around March 21st. The oldest historical record of the New Year is from the Achaemenid era at Persepolis; representatives of nations under Persian control are depicted bearing gifts for the king. Nowruz is still celebrated by many nations in the area that shared an Iranian heritage in the past.

Omar Khayyam (1048–1131): Prominent Iranian mathematician, astronomer, philosopher and poet. Omar Khayyam's poetry became a sensation in the 19th century when Edward Fitzgerald translated his collected works *Ruba'iyat* into English in 1859. The excerpts shown beside the paintings in *My Blue Canvas* are from English translations by Peter Avery and John Heath Stubbs, in the book, *The Ruba'iyat of Omar Khayyam,* published by Penguin Books in 1981.

Pasargadae Garden: Pasargadae is the first Achaemenid capital city built by Cyrus the Great and is his resting place. It is located in the north of Fars Province. The palace garden exhibits the ruins of a series of stone water channels and basins that divide the garden into four quarters. The design is the first known example of a Chahar Bagh garden that influenced later garden design in Iran and beyond.

Patience Stone: In Persian folklore the Patience Stone or *Sang-e sabour* is a magical black stone to which a person can confide and convey his/her problems. Eventually the stone would explode with all the sorrows of the person talking to it.

Persian Ice Flower: *Chimonantus* or Wintersweet originated in China but is also grown in Iran. It is a deciduous plant with small, strongly scented yellow or white flowers produced in early spring before the new leaves.

Pope, Arthur Upham (1881–1969): American educator, author and advocate of Persian art and architecture. Both Pope and his wife, Phyllis Ackerman are buried in Isfahan.

Qajar Dynasty (1779–1924): A ruling dynasty in Iran from Turkic origin. The Qajars united Iran, started some modernization, lost major territories to the Russians and the British, and made great achievements in the arts.

Qanat: Underground irrigation canals and aqua ducts. The technology was developed in Iran sometime in the first millennium BCE and spread to other areas.

Qibla: Muslims face Mecca during their daily prayers. *Qibla* means direction and it physically indicates the direction for praying towards Ka'aba, the holiest Muslim site.

Reza Shah Pahlavi (1878–1944): The founder of the Pahlavi Dynasty (1925–1979) was an army officer who rose through the ranks. He replaced the last Qajar monarch by an act of Parliament in 1925. He modernized Iran and implemented major reforms, but was ousted by the allied forces in 1941 when Iran was occupied during WWII.

Rumi, Jalal ad-Din Mohammad (1207–1273): Rumi was an Iranian poet, Islamic scholar and Sufi mystic. Written in Persian, his works have been translated into many languages. Rumi has been described as the most popular poet in America.

Sa'di Shirazi (1210–1291): Great master of Persian poetry and prose. His mausoleum in Shiraz, like that of Hafez, has become a pilgrim site for literature and art lovers in Iran.

Samovar: Russian metal container to heat and boil water for making tea. The *samovar* has become the traditional way for making tea in Iran and other countries in the region.

Sarv-e-naz: A species of cypress tree, an ornamental conifer widely propagated and planted in Iran, especially in Shiraz. Since ancient times the tree has been associated with significant symbolism including royalty, as evident in the stone carvings at Persepolis.

Sasanian Dynasty (224–650 CE): Guardians of a major Anahita temple in Balkh in modern Afghanistan, the Sasanians defeated the Parthians and formed the last great pre-Islamic Iranian empire. They rivalled Rome and ruled over Western Asia for over 400 years.

Sekanjebin: Sweet and sour syrup made with vinegar and mint and sweetened with honey or sugar. The syrup is served with water and ice and garnished with fresh mint leaves and cucumber.

Sepehri, Sohrab (1928–1980): A prominent poet and foremost Iranian modernist painter. His poetry uses nature imagery to convey his experiences, thoughts and concerns with human values. A long poem by Sohrab Sepehri, *Seday-e pay-e ab*, or *The Sound of the Footsteps of Water*, published in *Hasht Ketab*, by Tahouri publishers in Tehran in 1998, inspired the 36 paintings presented in *My Blue Canvas*. The excerpts shown beside the poems are from unpublished English translations by the author of this volume.

Setar: The meaning of the word in English is 'three strings'. It is the name of an Iranian stringed instrument, a member of the lute family, used in Iran and Central Asia. A fourth string was added to it more than two centuries ago.

Shab-e Yalda: An ancient pre-Islamic festival celebrating the winter solstice. The festival is celebrated on the eve of the first day of winter on the longest night of the year, and symbolizes the triumph of light over darkness. It is celebrated with family and friends, with festive foods, fresh and dried fruits and nuts, reading the poetry of Hafez, listening to music and playing traditional games.

Shafii Kadkani, Mohammad-Reza (born 1939): A prominent and very influential Iranian poet, literary critic, writer, editor, translator and university professor, his poetry deals with universal questions of life and the socio-political history of contemporary Iran. His poetry is inspired by images of nature and ancient Iranian culture and history.

Altogether, more than a hundred of Shafii Kadkani's poems have inspired Pari Azarm Motamedi's lingo-visual work of faithfully translating the poetry into English and then creating visual expressions of her interpretations of the poems. Some of the excerpts from the English translations and the visual depictions of the poems in *My Blue Canvas* have previously been published in a book titled *In the Mirror of the Stream, Selected Poems of Shafii Kadkani*, translations and paintings by Pari Azarm Motamedi, editor Alan Williams, published by Sokhan Publishers in Tehran in 2008. Sixteen other poems by Shafii Kadkani, in various volumes of the *Bukhara*, a literary journal published by Ali Dehbashi in Tehran, and *Ayeneh-ee baray-e sedaha*, *A Mirror for Sounds*, and *Hezareh Dovom-e Ahouy-e Kouhi*, *The Second Millenium of the Mountain Deer*, published by Sokhan Publishers, Tehran, 1997, also inspired some of the paintings in this book. The poetic excerpts, for these paintings are from previously unpublished translations by the author of *My Blue Canvas*. Altogether fifty-nine of the paintings inspired by Shafii Kadkani's poetry are presented in this volume.

Shahnameh: The national epic of Iran composed of 50,000 verses written by Abu'l-Qasem Ferdowsi. The work took over 30 years to create and was completed in the year 1010. It covers the legendary and semi-history of Iran from the first mythical king Gayumart, to the Arab conquest.

Sizdah be-dar: An Iranian festival celebrated on the 13th day of the first Iranian month marking the end of Nowruz celebrations in the spring. In pre-Islamic times the day was dedicated to a water deity. Following the ancient traditions celebrating nature and water, families spend the day in parks and outdoors, have a picnic, play games, dance and listen to music, and enjoy nature.

Sofreh-ye haft sin: Nowruz ceremonial table. Families gather around the *Sofreh-ye haft sin* to celebrate the arrival of Nowruz at the exact time the spring equinox occurs. The ceremonial spread has several symbolic items, herbs, greens and flowers and traditional foods and treats.

Tabarzin and Kashkul: Items traditionally carried by travelling dervishes. *Tabarzin* is an axe used in the past for chopping wood and protection. *Kashkul* is similar to the begging bowls used in Central Asia and is usually used for receiving alms.

Tar: Meaning 'string', *tar* is one of the most important stringed instruments in Iran and many neighbouring countries. The *tar* has six strings and a long neck with a double-bowl body made of mulberry wood. A thin lambskin covers the top of the bowl.

Zoroastrianism: One of the world's oldest monotheistic religions, Zoroastrianism was founded in ancient Iran by Prophet Zoroaster, around 3300 years ago and was the state religion in Iran prior to the arrival of Islam in the seventh century.